SYMBOLS IN THE CHURCH

SYMBOLS
IN
THE CHURCH

CARL VAN TREECK

and

ALOYSIUS CROFT, M.A.

THE BRUCE PUBLISHING COMPANY • MILWAUKEE

NIHIL OBSTAT:
JOHN F. MURPHY
Censor librorum

IMPRIMATUR:
✠ WILLIAM E. COUSINS
Archbishop of Milwaukee
October 4, 1960

All illustrations by
CARL VAN TREECK

Library of Congress Catalog Card Number: 36–8634
© 1960 THE BRUCE PUBLISHING COMPANY
MADE IN THE UNITED STATES OF AMERICA

PREFACE

THIS book is intended as a usable handbook for ecclesiastical artists and craftsmen of all sorts — painters, wood carvers, metalworkers, stained-glass workers, needle workers, and for others who are interested, theoretically or practically, in the decoration of churches and of liturgical objects — vestments, sacred vessels and the like. It attempts to present graphically practical ideas which they can apply in their work.

The single symbols shown herein have been collected from books and from original sources over a long period of years in the pursuit of liturgical art, especially stained-glass work, by the senior author. Many of them can be used for a number of purposes and while some few, especially very early ones referring to our Savior, may have little practical value now, they are included here because they may bring to the reader a sense of the depth and beauty of the older symbols. They have the further value of showing the tradition of the first centuries after Christ, during which the foundation of all Christian art was laid.

The symbols likewise have come from many sources from all the ages of Christianity — from small gems of the fourth and fifth centuries, from very large mosaics and frescoes, from medieval stained glass and tombstones, from the catacombs, and from Baroque engravings. The better material of more recent times is added also, and only the signs

5

devised in the ages of heraldry and as heraldic devices have, we think, properly, been omitted.

Since the book is not a history of symbolism nor a treatise on symbolism in general, footnotes, references, and other scholarly apparatus have been avoided. The history and philosophy of any symbol are presented only when it seemed necessary for an intelligent use of that particular symbol.

Furthermore, the book is not a complete collection of all Christian symbols; the field is too large to be covered in a volume the size of this one. Such limitations, of course, make it necessary to neglect many extremely interesting phases of the subject. However, the effort has been made, within proper bounds, to present only true symbols, and those which are the best and most authentic, and to deal with the subject in the correct spirit.

In order that the figures might be generally useful it was considered better not to retain their original artistic character. Consequently a general common form was sought for, and only for some of the material coming from the Middle Ages was a distinctive style used, the Gothic. It is as impossible, however, to prescind from all artistic style as it is to avoid a particular language in speech. Every design must have a particular character just as an idea that is expressed must be expressed in some language. At any rate, sheer naturalness has been avoided as the death of all liturgical art. The style in which the artist will reproduce the symbols finally will depend on the circumstances in which they are to be used. His own good judgment must guide him to the proper medium.

The explanations, like the symbols themselves, have been gathered from many sources. If any one book was used more than another it is *Christliche Symbole* by Dr. Schmid. In these explanations controversial points have been passed over wherever possible. That some of the symbols may be explained otherwise than we have done is, therefore, entirely possible. We have taken what seemed to be the best, most obvious, and the most traditional explanation.

It remains, then, only to hope that this work will fill a need; that artists and ecclesiastical craftsmen will find it useful; and that others also may find it interesting and may gain from it some inspiration to a deeper study of the beautiful picture language of the Church.

PREFACE TO THE SECOND EDITION

IN THE quarter-century which has passed since this book was written, there has been a marvelous advance in the use of Christian symbols — a result, in large part, of the growth of the liturgical spirit, with its return to the living past. A generation of young artists has learned to use, combine, and adapt the ancient symbols to the new needs.

That this book will still serve the purpose for which it was originally intended, however, seems clear from the many requests received for information on the basic symbols. To impart such information was the aim of the authors; to the users of the book themselves must be left the task of applying the symbols with imagination and artistry.

Relatively few material changes have been made in the present edition. The text has been altered somewhat, a few figures have been dropped, and the drawings have been rearranged so that the book will be, we hope, more attractive and more readily usable.

CONTENTS

11

SYMBOLS IN THE CHURCH

1. SYMBOLISM AND SYMBOLS

THE exact meaning of the word *symbol* has become somewhat obscured through the centuries, so that now the term is applied more or less indiscriminately to types, figures, allegories, and attributes, as well as to symbols proper.

The word *symbol* is derived from two Greek words, *syn* meaning "together," "with," and *ballein,* "to throw." The symbol, then, as the word implies, is a throwing together or combination of an abstract idea and a visible sign — the latter representing the former. Strictly speaking, therefore, any such sign — an attitude or position of the hand, a number, a representation either painted or sculptured — may be a symbol; the movements and positions of the priest's hands during the sacred liturgy, for example, are symbolic in the highest sense.

Symbolism has some part in all genuine art and it may be said that Christian art must of necessity be symbolic, since in art there is always the element of the supernatural — an

15

element that cannot be represented directly. And symbolism did actually play a most important role in Christian art up to the time when the spirit of the Renaissance, with its flattering of the sensual in man, robbed this art of its deepest meaning. The artists of the earlier centuries had too much respect, for example, for the divine and supernatural to represent our divine Lord or the saints by merely human and natural figures. What is often considered by some as mere stylistic exaggeration in these early works of art, is this very element of symbolization.

Since it is the purpose of this book to present to the artist and to others a clear idea of the designs proper for the decoration of vestments and other liturgical objects, as well as of churches, it will be necessary to distinguish between symbols and those other figures which are often improperly termed symbols. The cross, for example, so often seen, is a symbol of our faith in the salvific death of our Savior, which is the basis of the whole Christian belief; but the representation of the Savior crucified, the crucifix, is not a symbol but purely a picture, although this picture may have symbolic elements. Again, the brazen serpent erected by Moses in the desert is no symbol as long as it is represented as belonging to the Old Testament; it is a *prototype*, a figure of something yet to come.

The *attribute* also is often confused with the symbol. The attribute, as the name implies, is something added to a particular figure to distinguish it from others. It is a thing naturally connected with some event, or virtue, or dignity, or condition in the life of the person represented, or with the manner of his death. It is usually shown in connection with a representation of the person or his symbol: for example, the winged man is the symbol of the evangelist, St. Matthew, but when St. Matthew himself is represented in connection with the winged man, this latter is no longer his symbol,

16

but an attribute. Thus also, the attributes of St. James the Less, the saw, and of St. Paul, the sword, which indicate the manner of their deaths, are when shown alone not symbols of these saints but merely a saw and a sword. Examples of the attribute might be multiplied, but these are sufficient to explain its nature.

These three, the symbol, the prototype, and the attribute, are in a sense related, but they should not be confused in use. The present book is concerned only with symbols, and hence figures of the others are not given.

There are some abstract ideas, such as temperance, fortitude, folly, for which, because of their very nature, it is difficult to find intelligible symbols. Possibly the easiest and most appropriate way of representing such ideas is through the use of flower symbols combined with pertinent quotations. The medieval artists solved the problem by representing a female figure bearing a scroll upon which appeared the name of the virtue.

Finally, it is not possible to give any hard-and-fast rules for the use of symbols. Rules, of course, there are, but these appear more in the breach than in the observance. There are certain general counsels, however, which may well be given. In the first place, symbols should not be used merely because they are symbols. The decoration of church walls or windows must not consist of a collection of archaeological curiosities. Obviously a mosaic floor must receive different treatment from that given a sanctuary lamp or a window. In general the use of symbols should aim to impart a liturgical spirit to the decoration of sacred things, and those symbols and combinations of symbols should be chosen which best conduce to this end. Some of them can be shown in series, others must stand alone. Serious study and good taste, coupled with religious sense, will dictate the proper symbols to use in particular cases.

17

It is necessary, in the second place, to guard against overloading any decoration with symbols. Overrich use of symbolic designs will not make an artistic work of something that is weak in itself. For the first Christians symbols served as a secret language, but in our times this is no longer true. They are used now to give to liturgical objects a decoration in harmony with their character and to suggest the truths of the Faith to those who behold them. The use of symbols is itself a secondary matter: artistic fitness and liturgical correctness are the primary requisites. Symbols, then, are no retriever of poor art: they can only raise to a higher plane a work that is already good.

Finally, it is important to keep a logical order in the use of symbols, that is, to take all the designs in one series or on one object from one period of art, and to use those which are prompted by one viewpoint. There is no logic in combining the early Christian ☧ with the medieval Gothic IHC. Strict distinction should be made between the venerable symbols coming from the first years of the Christian era, with their profound religious sense and their tradition leading back to the early martyrs, and the medieval symbols, which are certainly also beautiful, but which were designed chiefly as decorations. Order and fitness must be observed in this as in all things.

THE NIMBUS

The nimbus takes its origin from nature. In certain lights and about certain substances there often appears the phenomenon of a circle of light seemingly emanating from the substance. The nimbus, then, was taken even prior to the Christian era as a sign of dignity or light emanating from persons of exalted station or character. The Roman emperors

18

and empresses were represented with a rayed fillet about their heads and later the emperors wore a rayed crown. In early Christian times the nimbus retained this same significance, and in some mosaics the Byzantine emperors are distinguished by the nimbus while figures of saints in the same picture are not distinguished in any way. A notable example of this is the mosaic in the Church of St. Vitale at Ravenna, showing the Emperor Justinian with a retinue of clerics among whom is St. Maximian. This usage continued as late as Carolingian times. There are pictures from that time, of angels and saints, in which the nimbus is not shown. During this same period living persons, prelates and other dignitaries, civil and ecclesiastical, were sometimes portrayed with a square nimbus, usually gray in color. A mosaic in the Basilica of Demetrius in Saloniki, dating from about the seventh century, shows a figure having this square nimbus.

Today the nimbus is taken as a sign of divinity, or of the sanctity of persons who are raised above their fellows by grace. It is used not only on representations of the Persons of the Most Blessed Trinity but on their symbols as well, and upon representations of angels and saints.

In the nimbus used to distinguish the divine Persons, especially the divine Savior, and their symbols (for example, the Lamb, the hand), there is usually a cross of which generally only three beams are visible. The question is sometimes raised whether these beams are actually those of a cross with the fourth hidden, or whether they are properly only three and refer to the Holy Trinity. However, since there are pictures in which all four beams are visible, it seems safe to dismiss the Trinity-symbol theory. The beams are sometimes visible in the form of rays, and not seldom the rays alone (without the circle) are seen.

Again, as a rule the color of the nimbus is gold, but not

19

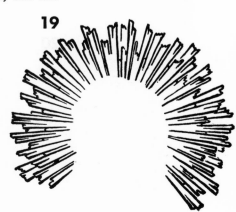

necessarily. There are medieval pictures, miniatures, stained glass, and frescoes, in which different colored nimbuses are found for different figures. Red, blue, green, and gold nimbuses may appear in the same picture. There is hardly a liturgical reason for this, or even a symbolic one; it seems to be merely a matter of color harmony and decoration. Many of them are richly decorated according to the various styles, and are usually circles, although in some works, of Giotto for example (1266–1337), the broken circle — octagon or many-sided figure — is sometimes found.

During the period of renaissance and humanistic and naturalistic influence art lost a great deal of the dignity and remoteness that characterized it in the Middle Ages. In the later period the nimbus was not always used and then only when it was in harmony with the naturalistic and artistic concept. It never became an integral part of the composition but remained something superimposed. When shown at all it consisted, as a rule, of a very few gold rays or a circle directly above the head, or merely of a lightening of the background above the head.

In the Middle Ages and later, too, especially in the seventeenth and eighteenth centuries, under Baroque influence, there developed another nimbus, the glory or mandorla as it is called. This is an enlarged nimbus usually of gold which envelops the whole body. It implies the notion of glory, and is used for the Persons of the Holy Trinity, particularly for the Savior, and also for the Blessed Virgin Mary. The glory as it was developed in the Baroque was an integral part of the decoration. It is used much today, but generally with somewhat less prominence than before. For an example see the headpiece for Chapter 2.

20

2. THE MOST HOLY TRINITY

IN VIEW of the central place which the doctrine of the Most
Holy Trinity holds in the Christian religion, it is somewhat
surprising to find that symbols of the Blessed Trinity were
extremely uncommon in the early ages of Christianity. The
doctrine was certainly well defined in the first years of this
era, and many clear statements concerning it are found in
the writings of the early Fathers, such as St. Gregory
(Thaumaturgus), Tertullian, and others. The Council of
Nicaea (325), when it defined the place of the three divine
Persons in the Blessed Trinity, was teaching no new doctrine.
However, with the exception of that shown on page 23 (**.3.**),
no early symbols have been brought to light.

While there was no such dearth of symbols in the Middle
Ages, still, aside from a few geometrical forms taken from
the architecture of the time, there is little that is useful for
the decorator today. Furthermore, these geometrical forms

21

may have been intended originally as aids to explaining the Holy Trinity rather than as symbols of the three divine Persons in one Godhead. In general they convey no idea whatever of divinity, and the old artists, recognizing this, sometimes added explanatory inscriptions. It is even possible that these devices were not originally designed to represent the theological idea of the Trinity, but were simply ornamental motifs to which the symbolical meaning was later added. But whatever their original purpose, they are considered today as proper symbols.

These geometrical symbols are the equilateral triangle, the trefoil, and the interlaced circles of equal size, and numerous variations of these basic forms, such as the shamrock: all are based upon the number three. To them may be added the circle as the symbol of infinity.

Since late Renaissance times, the all-seeing eye has also been taken to symbolize the Holy Trinity. This application is entirely proper since there is no reason for using the eye exclusively to symbolize God the Father. However, when it is referred to the Blessed Trinity, it must be placed within an equilateral triangle; from the sides of this triangle rays may come, although they are not essential to the meaning of the symbol. The names of God found in the Old Testament, written in Hebrew and placed in an equilateral triangle, are also found in this connection.

The headpiece shows a representation of the Most Blessed Trinity common during the Middle Ages and often appropriately used today as an altarpiece. Because it is representative rather than symbolical it is really outside the sphere of this book, but it was thought well to include it because of its interesting and well-rounded composition. It shows God the Father, enthroned and wearing the royal crown (sometimes a tiara), supporting upon His knees the crucified Christ above whose head hovers the Holy Spirit, symbolized by the dove.

22

The whole is an understandable and inspiring attempt at representing the Trinity.

Somewhat in the same spirit and showing the same mingling of picturization and symbolization is an altarpiece ordered in 1453, for a monastery chapel in Italy. The terms of the contract which is still extant, require that: "First there shall be the form of Paradise, and in this Paradise shall be the Holy Trinity, and between the Father and the Son shall be no difference and the Holy Spirit in the form of a dove. . . ."[1]

It may be well to note that a symbol of the Trinity sometimes mentioned in books on symbolism, the single head with three faces, is forbidden by the Church.

EXPLANATION OF SYMBOLS

.3. The Christogram (☧) and the alpha and omega placed within an equilateral triangle, come from very early times, and may be considered as the first symbols of the Holy Trinity. We cannot be certain, however, that in early representations the symbol as a whole actually refers to the Trinity as such. It would seem more probable that it represents the Savior as a member of the Holy Trinity since there is no specific reference to the other two divine Persons.

.4. A trefoil formed of interlacing lines (the three divine Persons) in which the circle (unity and infinity) is incorporated.

.5. The trefoil: the three leaves (three divine Persons) form one figure (one God). Quite often an equilateral triangle or a circle (infinity) is added.

.6. Three circles of equal size (three divine Persons having no beginning and no end, and co-equal) are interlaced so as to form one figure (one God). The inscription explain-

---

[1] Also mentioned in A. de Bles, *How to Distinguish the Saints in Art* (New York: Art Culture Publications, Inc., 1925).

.3.

.4.

.5.

.6.

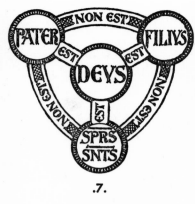

.7.

.8.

.9.

ing the symbol is found in some, though not all, originals of the Middle Ages, and is not necessary.

.7. Figure taken from a woodcut of the sixteenth century and also found on stained glass of that time. It explains itself. It is an interesting theological formula rather than a symbol. We include it here merely because of its ingenuity and explanatory value.

.8. St. Patrick is said to have used the shamrock in explaining to the pagan Irish the idea of the Holy Trinity. Of all the symbols that have for their purpose to explain a doctrine, this one has been most cherished by tradition. It affords the craftsman much more opportunity for development of composition than do the geometrical designs.

.9. Three burning candles (three divine Persons) are molded into one (the Godhead).

.10. A single candle (the Godhead) is held by a candlestick having three legs (three divine Persons).

.11. An equilateral triangle formed by three fishes is often used to symbolize the Holy Trinity, especially in the decoration of objects used in baptism. Some authorities indeed see in this device a symbol only of baptism.

If it is true, however, that this device comes from very early times, perhaps both meanings are correct. It may mean that in the name of the Holy Trinity we should become like our Leader, Christ (see explanation of fish, p. 35 f.). The other explanations may be that baptism in the name of the Holy Trinity, takes us like fish from the water of sin.

24

.10.

.11.

3. GOD THE FATHER

It is not difficult to understand that most of the symbols of God the Father will be drawn from the Old Testament. Surrounded as they were by pagan neighbors, and inclined to polytheism, the Jews were not prepared to receive the fullness of revelation concerning the Godhead. It was the Person of the Father who revealed Himself to them, and not until the work of His divine Son was under way on earth, was the Blessed Trinity clearly and openly revealed. But the Old Testament does show forth the Father, and to it can be traced most of the ideas symbolized.

The earliest Christian symbols of God the Father are in the form of the *Dextera Domini*, the right hand of the Lord, so often mentioned in Scripture. The hand is usually shown coming from a cloud which sometimes seems to conceal the rest of the human figure. At other times the cloud is indicated only faintly or even omitted entirely. It is very unusual

25

to find the hand pictured as open: Usually the thumb and the first two fingers are extended in the position of blessing. Since medieval times the hand has been surrounded by a rayed nimbus in the form used generally for figures and symbols of the divine Persons (see p. 19). The position of the hand, upright, sideward, or extended downward, is merely a matter of composition or usage, and has no effect on the meaning of the symbol.

One picture of the Baptism of Christ, by Andrea de Verrocchio, dating from the early Italian Renaissance period, symbolizes God the Father by two outstretched hands from which a dove, the Holy Spirit, is gently descending.

In the sixteenth century the all-seeing eye came into use in place of the hand. The eye is always enclosed within a triangle, which need not be equilateral, and which is usually surrounded by rays.

There is a difference between these two devices which should be recognized in their use. As a symbol of the Deity, above a high altar, for instance, in which God is represented in all His power and majesty, the all-seeing eye is very appropriate. On the other hand, in connection with some particular act such as the baptism of our Savior, or the creation of man, the hand is more frequently found.

Besides these two symbols, as has been said in the chapter on the Holy Trinity, God the Father is also symbolized by the names given Him in the Old Testament, written in Hebrew and surrounded by rays or placed in a triangle.

The headpiece shows the Greek form of the name of God taken from Exodus (3:14): "I am who am." This was the commonly accepted Old Testament name for God — *Jaweh* — the name which the Jews venerated above all the names of God.

There is no representation in human form of the first Per-

26

.12.

.13.

son of the Holy Trinity that dates from the first centuries, a fact due to the strong Jewish tradition, still alive in the Church, which would scarcely allow the pronunciation of the Name of God, not to mention pictorial representation. Certainly, too, it is evidence of the deep reverence for God among the early Christians.

EXPLANATION OF SYMBOLS

.12. Shows the extended hand coming from the cloud. The rays emanating from the hand symbolize blessings.

.13.–.14. The hand with fingers extended in benediction. The hand is surrounded by the cruciform nimbus, peculiar to representations and symbols of the divine Persons.

.15. The name *Jaweh* in Hebrew characters. Since the Hebrew alphabet lacks vowels, this word has only four letters and is called the Tetragrammaton. During the sixteenth and seventeenth centuries this symbol was considered miraculous.

.16. The all-seeing eye in a triangle from the sides of which emanate rays.

.17. The Hebrew characters for the word *Adonai*, "the Lord," or better, "my Lord."

.18. *El Shaddai* — the Almighty.

27

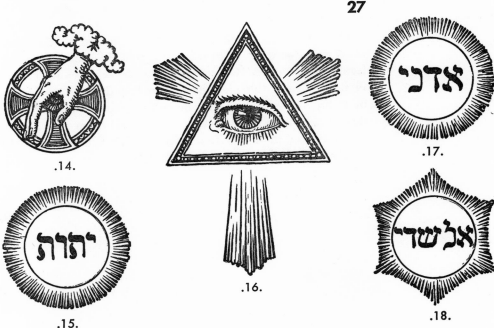

.14.

.17.

.16.

.15.

.18.

4. GOD THE SON

1

THE most prolific and most engaging growth of symbolism centered about the person of our Savior, Jesus Christ. Human ingenuity rose to its greatest heights in forming suitable and worthy figures of this Most Beautiful of the sons of men. But before taking up in detail this phase of the subject, it will be interesting and helpful to consider briefly the spirit in which the art of different periods depicted our divine Lord.

The art of the first centuries was dominated by the spirit of classic times, a spirit that was chiefly Hellenistic and frankly humanistic. Its beauty was a physical beauty having in it little or nothing of the spiritual, and therefore having in it no room for suffering or sorrow. Hence we find that during this period the Savior was pictured often as a beautiful youth; or in scenes from His life which manifested His power, His bounty, His glory. It was this spirit, too, that

28

applied to Him at times the concepts of the pagan gods, picturing Him, for example, in the form of Orpheus as the Good Shepherd (see headpiece). During this period our Lord was shown as the Lord of nature, the Wonderworker, the Giver of the Law. As early as the third or fourth century there were pictures of the triumphal entry into Jerusalem and of the Miracle at Cana. But there is scarcely any representation, dating from this time, of the scourging or any other stage of the passion. The Crucifixion on the door of the Church of St. Sabina at Rome, mentioned often in books on early Christian art, dates, it is true, from the fifth century, but it is the one notable exception to the rule.

This classical spirit extended up to the beginning of the Middle Ages, when a different concept gradually arose. From this time on it became the custom to represent the Savior with beard and flowing locks, much as we see Him pictured today. The Christ Child was represented with a face full of wisdom and sometimes of age. The extreme religious feeling of this period, too, succeeded in representing the sufferings of the Savior with a depth and awfulness that is heart-rending — a fact well borne out by the Isenheimer Altar of Matthias Gruenewald, at Colmar, France. Indeed, this painting represents the spirit of medieval art at its zenith.

The beginning of the Renaissance — roughly, about the fourteenth century in Italy, but in the North as late as the sixteenth century — marked the third period of Christian art. This movement, with its reversion to the classical spirit, did away with much of the intense feeling of the medieval representations of our divine Lord. Emphasis shifted from depth and strength to sweetness and beauty of form and composition — from the spiritual to the material and physical. This emphasis on material perfection, accepted in our own times and influenced by our own peculiar superficiality, has degenerated into mere prettiness. The result is to be seen in

29

such works as those of Hoffmann and Plockhorst — works which certainly possess beauty but which are distinctly humanistic and altogether un-Catholic. It is regrettable that the art of our time follows so closely the Renaissance ideal, that it accepts as its models the sweetness of Perugino and Raphael, neglecting the other high artistic qualities of these masters, and ignoring altogether the tremendous power of the medieval artists such as Giotto.

There is one more point to be noted before taking up the consideration proper of the symbols of our Lord. During the first ten centuries there were, with some few exceptions, no pictures showing our Blessed Savior unclothed, because the unclothed body of the divine Person was considered too sacred to be profaned by the gaze of mortal eyes.

2

Speaking specifically of the symbols of our Lord, it may seem very strange that the most common of all Christian signs, the cross, was not known as a symbol much before the fifth century. It was, however, often shown in a veiled way — what we might call the disguised or hidden cross, known to archaeologists as the *crux dissimulata*. As early as the second century the Christians were signing themselves with the cross as a mark of identification among themselves and as a blessing. But, despite this, the cross was not used as we use it, as a symbol of our faith and principles. Reasons for this fact are not far to seek: there was, for one, the necessity of avoiding betrayal to enemies of the Faith who might be those of one's own household; besides, the cross was, as St. Paul said (1 Cor. 1:23), "unto the Jews a stumbling block, and unto the Gentiles foolishness," and could not be too openly displayed lest it repulse even well-meaning friends. This last was true even after the persecutions had ceased.

Hence, the Christians used, as has been said, the *crux dissimulata,* a device that had a number of forms, the most common of which was the anchor.

The anchor has been for many ages the symbol of hope; the Christians based their hope in the saving merits of Jesus Christ, and thus, very appropriately, the anchor came to symbolize the Savior. And the initiated saw in its upright bar and transverse beam the figure of the cross.

Another device which may also have been a veiled cross, is the Christogram, formed by the crossing of the P or I by the X. This symbol is explained later in this chapter.

The cross itself, in the form we know it today, probably did not come into general use until late in the fourth century. But once popularized it was so adorned and modified that there are literally dozens of different kinds of crosses, varying in form, length of beam, and decoration. It is to little purpose to enter here on an explanation of these various cross-forms, since most of them convey no symbolical idea, and are mere heraldic devices interesting now only for decorative purposes. One form, however, the Celtic cross, has considerable artistic, historical, and cultural significance. This is particularly beautiful and artistic, and presents less severe lines than the plain Latin cross. It is found as early as the tenth century, usually in stone, and richly embellished with figures and delicate symbolic tracery.

The *crux gemmata* which is not a particular form, but simply an ornamented Latin cross, took its origin in about the fifth century from the very natural desire on the part of Christians to honor the sign of the world's redemption. Precious metals and gems were used as ornamentation; and in painting, these were represented in brilliant colors. Sometimes the cross was shown with flowers growing from its base. When St. John Chrysostom (347–407) was upholding Catholic doctrine against the Arians, he carried in procession

31

a cross of silver, bearing on its arms lighted candles (to represent Christ the Light of the World) and depending from the arms the alpha and omega (A and Ω), the symbols of Christ's divinity. There are examples too of the cross in form of a tree (see *Pange Lingua*, by Venantius Fortunatus, A.D. 606). The decorated cross remained in common use up to the eleventh or twelfth century, and the term *crux gemmata* is used by archaeologists in reference only to the jeweled and ornamented crosses up to that time. However, the decorated cross is not rare today; nearly every pectoral cross is a *crux gemmata*.

The device most often used in ancient times was the Greek monogram of Christ, commonly called the Christogram and mentioned previously. To facilitate the understanding of this symbol, a few remarks on the use of the Greek letters are in place.

At the time of the founding of Christianity Greek culture held sway over a large portion of the then civilized western world. The Latin, of course, was the common language, but Greek was also quite universally understood and spoken. In the East, as a result of the conquests of Alexander the Great, the Greek language was known and used very commonly, even among the Jews; and thus it is that three of the four Gospels were written, not in Aramaic, Hebrew, or Latin, but in Greek. Greek, then, was the language in which the Faith was introduced into Rome from the East, and it remained, until about the year 250, the language of Christianity. Now, the Greek translation of the Hebrew name *Joshua* — Jesus — is written in capital letters, IHCOUC, and the word *Christ* (which means anointed) XPICTOC. (These are also written IHΣOUΣ XPIΣTOΣ — the difference being in the two forms of sigma, C and Σ; in liturgical work the former is preferred.) Thus, in the Christogram there may be either the first two letters of the word XPICTOC com-

32

bined to form ✗, or the initial letters of the words IHCOUC XPICTOC forming ✗.

This sign took its popularity from an incident connected with the legalization of Christianity. In the year 312, Constantine the Great, Augustus of the West, was about to join battle with Maxentius, Augustus of the East, at the Milvian bridge. Shortly before the battle, Constantine had some sort of religious experience which turned him toward the God of the Christians. He is commonly said to have seen in the heavens a sign and the words EN TOYTΩ NIKA (*En touto nika*) "In This Sign (You Shall) Conquer." He ordered a standard to be made bearing the device ✗, and his army, fighting under the standard of Christ, was victorious. Shortly after this in A.D. 313, Constantine and Licinius, as joint emperors, published the so-called "Edict of Toleration," giving the Christian Church the legal right to exist. The standard which the Roman legions carried was called the *Labarum* (sometimes applied incorrectly to the sign ✗ alone), and this *labarum* of Constantine is found represented on many coins of the late Roman era. Christians, however, had used the Christogram very early. It was inscribed upon tombstones in the catacombs just as we inscribe a cross. It was used on seal rings, and later, in the fourth century, was painted even on the shields of the legionaries.

The forms ✗ and ✗ are practically contemporary. In the beginning the letters alone were used, but as time went on the symbols of eternity or infinity — a circle or alpha omega (AΩ) — were added, as a protest against the Arian denial of Christ's divinity; sometimes a peacock was added as the symbol of immortality.

In their symbolic connection, the letters AΩ (alpha and omega) are interesting. They are the most proper, dignified, and most exclusively Christian of all symbols of the divinity or eternity. Their use takes its origin from the Apocalypse

.19.

The labarum
of Constantine

33

(1:8): "I am the Alpha and Omega, the beginning and the end, saith the Lord God. . . ." They are found written variously as ΑΩ, the majuscules, or αω, the minuscules. At times, too, they are written incorrectly AO — incorrectly because the O (omicron), while equivalent as is the Ω to the English O, is not the last letter of the Greek alphabet.

It should be noted that these letters should always be joined with some other symbol to give them meaning. Alone they are merely two letters of the Greek alphabet. The peacock, too, by itself represents immortality and the circle infinity, but only in connection with some symbol of the Savior do they represent *His* immortality and infinity. The custom of using these signs alone arose only in recent centuries; in the classic periods of symbolism they are always seen in connection with other symbols. The circle, sometimes formed by a snake holding its tail in the mouth, and the peacock are, unlike the alpha and omega, of pagan origin. The latter was the symbol of the divinity of the Roman pagan empresses, as the eagle was of the emperors.

As has been said, the Christogram was the symbol seen most commonly in the ancient Church. In the Middle Ages, however, especially in the fourteenth, fifteenth, and sixteenth centuries a new device took its place — the monogram of Jesus, IHS. This symbol, of course, has not the liturgical importance of the older one which was replaced by the cross as the symbol and sign of the Christian faith.

This monogram of Jesus is formed — or more properly contracted — from the Greek IHCOYC (*Iesous*) "Jesus." It consists of the first two and the last letter of this word, and above it the medieval orthographers placed the ⌒, the contraction sign. When, as most often happened, the Gothic letters were used, the letters appeared thus ιhc; then, the contraction mark combined with the perpendicular line of the eta formed a cross, and gave to the whole symbol a much

34

wider significance. The device, besides being full of religious meaning, afforded to the medieval artists a splendid opportunity for creating graceful and richly ornamented compositions.

As time went on, knowledge of the Greek tongue became more rare and the original significance of this symbol was lost. The Greek C was changed to the Latin S. The meaning of these letters, looking so much like the Latin I, h, and s, was sought, and finally found in the words *Jesus Hominum Salvator* — "Jesus the Savior of men."

Again it was explained as the initial letters of the phrase *in hoc signo* (EN TOYTΩ NIKA), because while the letters might be changed to the Roman capitals, the cross, first formed accidentally by the contraction sign and the upper part of the h, was kept, resting upon the bar of the H, thus ⊞. Often, too, the phrase was completed by the addition of v (for *vinces*, NIKA), formed sometimes from the nails of the crucifixion. This last is not always shown, but the cross is very seldom omitted, and the whole symbol may be surrounded by rays.

Besides the Latin explanation of this symbol, there are German and English ones as well. The Germans derive the letters from the words *Jesus, Heiland, Seligmacher*, and the English, from "I have suffered." As has been seen, none of these explanations are historically correct, yet they have behind them the tradition of centuries, and none of them offends against doctrine. For these reasons, and because today the original meaning has been all but forgotten, they should be treated with a certain respect.

From these symbols, originating from more or less natural sources, we pass to one that seems to us today to be rather strange. The fish, as the symbol of the Holy Name of Jesus, is of more complicated origin than the others. If it seems strange and difficult of interpretation to us, it was just as

35

complicated to the uninitiated of the early days, and precisely in this fact lay its great usefulness for the early Christians.

As an acrostic the Greek word for fish, IXΘYC, yields the initial letters of the words IHCOYC XPICTOC ΘEOY YIOC CΩTHP — "Jesus Christ, Son of God, Savior." A symbol so simple and meaningless in itself, and yet having so much significance to those who knew, could not but serve as a sign in a multitude of ways. And so it did. The fish is a common sign in the catacombs; it was depicted in murals and engravings. Small images of fish made of wood or other materials, sometimes inscribed with the word CΩCEIC (soseis), "you will save," were carried by the Christians much as we carry crucifixes or medals. In many ways it served as a sign of identification among friends, and a safeguard against enemies.

It is difficult to realize how the understanding of a symbol so bound up with the early ages of the Faith could have been lost. That it has been lost, however, is the fact; although, in recent years, happily, the symbol is coming back into more frequent use. There is a sacred atmosphere surrounding this ancient sign that can never be acquired by the later and more sentimental symbols.

Before leaving this symbol it is necessary, too, to note the two meanings derived from it. First of all, as we have seen, the fish symbolizes the Savior; but it may also symbolize the faithful, who must become like to their Redeemer, Christ Jesus. Tertullian, writing on baptism, bears out this idea when he says: "We are little fishes, and like our Fish, Jesus Christ, we are born in the water; we are not saved otherwise than by remaining in the water."* St. Matthew also hints at it in his Gospel (4:19).

One of the most easily understood, and most meaningful

---

*"Nos pisciculi, secundum Ἰχθύν nostrum Jesum Christum, in aqua nascimur; nec aliter quam in aqua permanendo salvi sumus" (De Baptismo, I).

36

symbols of our Blessed Lord is the Lamb. Its origin can be traced directly to the Gospels, and even to the Old Testament where the Christ is spoken of as "a lamb" (Isa. 53:7). The references to the lamb in the liturgy are numerous, and we need cite only the *Agnus Dei* of the Mass.

The use of the lamb as a symbol of Christ goes back as far as that of the Christogram or the fish. It is a common representation in the catacombs — not always indeed with the same details as today, but in substantially the same way. At first the lamb was usually not depicted with the nimbus, but sometimes bore the Christogram on its head. Later on this was generally replaced by the nimbus. Again the lamb might be lying, or standing — sometimes on a book with seven seals (see Apoc. 5:1). At times, too, it was shown with the banner of Easter — a white pennant bearing a red cross and attached to a cruciform staff. This banner, variously called the Easter banner or the Resurrection banner, is interesting in its own right and merits a few words. A white pennant is sometimes taken as the symbol of the body of Christ. This pennant, affixed to the cruciform standard represents the death on the cross through which the risen Christ brought salvation to mankind.

To return to the lamb; as with the fish, so, too, more than one lamb represents the faithful; "feed My lambs, feed My sheep." The twelve Apostles, also, are sometimes represented as twelve lambs, arranged six on each side of a single lamb (cf. headpiece, Chap. 7) identified as Christ by either the Christogram or the cruciform nimbus (cf. section on the nimbus). The use of the lamb in these connections is not rare and because of its antiquity, solid scriptural basis, and decorative qualities will appeal to all those interested in symbolism.

The four classical symbols of our Savior, then, are the disguised cross, the Christogram, the fish, and the lamb. There

37

.20.

.21.

.22.

.23.

.24.

.25.

were others, of course, in the early times, such as the figure of Orpheus, but to enter into their explanation would be beyond the limits of this work. The Middle Ages and the last centuries have given a few important new ideas. The instruments of the passion, for instance, were used at that time — and are used today correctly — by showing them in a series.

Another important new symbol springs from the veneration of the Sacred Heart so popular of late years. It must be noted, however, that, according to a decree of the Sacred Congregation of Rites (Sept. 12, 1857), without the permission of the Ordinary, the Heart alone, that is, apart from the figure of Christ, must not be shown on the main altar. The Heart, where used, may bear the wound, flames, and thorns (S. C. Inq., Jan. 3, 1891). There is nothing prohibiting the use of the Heart in small pictures, or in the decoration of church walls and windows, and properly used it may be a means not only of symbolic decoration, but of real edification. It demands care and taste in handling, however, and without this it were better left alone.

38

.26.

.20. An anchor cross.

.21. The *crux ansata.*

.22. A tau cross, or *crux commissa.*

.23. An anchor cross formed from the letters I X.

.24. The patriarchal or archiepiscopal cross.

.25. The papal cross, carried in processions in which the Holy Father takes part.

.26. A richly ornamented cross (*crux gemmata*) of the usual proportions of the Latin cross (the *crux immissa*). Neither the candles nor the alpha — omega are essential features of this form. This drawing is an adaptation from a fresco in the catacomb of Pontianus.

.27. A cross standing on three steps, upon each of which the name of one of the theological virtues is sometimes written. This is found quite often in oriental Christian decoration, with or without the inscriptions.

.27.

.28. A Celtic cross, sometimes called a "wheel cross" because of the circle connecting the beams.

.28.

.29. — .30. — .31. Various forms of the Christogram. In Figure .30. the chi has the form of a cross, made by a transverse stroke across the P.

.32. Christogram, the X of which is formed by the palms signifying victory.

.33. Christogram flanked by palms of victory.

.29.

39

.33.

.32.

.30.

.31.

.34.

.35.

.36.

.37.

.34. The letters in this monogram are the Greek letters X P N. The X is formed by crossing the N with the perpendicular stroke of the P. The words from which these letters are taken are XPICTOC NIKA (*Christos Nika*) — "Christ conquers." The symbol has practically the same significance as the monogram with the palms.

.35. The monogram I X is taken from the words IHCOYC XPICTOC (*Iesous Christos*) — "Jesus Christ."

.36. The monogram of Jesus Christ, imposed upon a cross, the whole within a circle. The meaning of the symbol is Jesus Christ (I X) crucified (the cross) eternal God (the circle of eternity).

.37. A contraction of the word IHCOUC (*Iesous*). The mark over the letters is the sign of contraction.

.38. The contraction of the word XPICTOC (*Christos*).

.39. The fish with the inscription IXΘYC (*ichthys*) to be read as an acrostic (see p. 36).

.40. to .46. Various ornamental arrangements of the IHS monogram in Gothic style. **.45.** is a contraction of the word XPICTOC (*Christos*).

.47. A device taken from a ringstone. The fact that the monogram cuts through the fish is noteworthy. Without doubt it signifies death. The whole is a symbol of the sacrificed Savior.

40

.38.

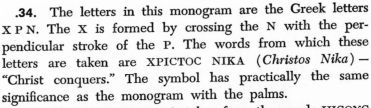

IXΘYC

.39.

.40.

.41.

.42.

.43.

.44.

.45.

.46.

.47.

.48.

.49.

.50.

.48. The fish, representing the Savior, brings the cross, on the arm of which rests a dove carrying the olive branch of peace, to the faithful, the lamb.

.49. From one side of the anchor hangs a fish, while on the other side is another fish free of the anchor, but bearing the word CΩCEIC (*soseis*) — "you will save (me)." It represents the desire of the world for salvation through the cross (cf. **.50.**).

.50. Two fish, representing the faithful, are attached to the anchor. The symbol represents the faithful saved by the cross.

.51. An anchor, concealed cross, with the fish twined about it. The inscription reads ΕΠΙΤΥΝΧΑΝΟΥ (*epitynchanou*) — "take." The symbol represents the crucified Savior. It is taken from a ringstone.

.52. The Christogram enthroned upon a platform to which three steps lead, and flanked by palms. The symbol represents the Savior enthroned and triumphant. From the catacombs.

.53. The Lamb of God, as the Good Shepherd. The palm beside the Lamb represents a shepherd's crook which has blossomed, symbolizing eternal life. Upon the blossomed crook hangs a vessel in which the Lamb brings His own blood to the faithful.

42

ΕΠΙΤΥΝ XΑΝΟΥ

.51.

.54. This symbol is impressed upon the host used in the Byzantine liturgy, by Orthodox and Catholics alike. The circle represents eternity; the square, the temporal character of the world; the contractions I C X C, and the word NIKA, "Jesus Christ conquers."

.55. This is taken from a cut stone. The faithful, symbolized by the doves, look for salvation to the crucified Savior, the Christogram and alpha and omega. The serpent recalls the brass serpent which Moses set up in the desert, for the healing of his people.

.56. A cross formed by the words ΦΩϹ ΖΩΗ (*Phos Zoe*) — "the light," "life." The meaning is that Christ is the light and life of the world. Taken from a pyx of the eighth or ninth century.

.57. A labarum or standard. The banner refers to the body of Christ as the Christogram implies. The serpent represents sin conquered by the Savior on the cross. Christ crucified is the hope of the people, *Spes Publica*. This figure is taken from a coin of Constantine the Great.

43

.52.

.53.

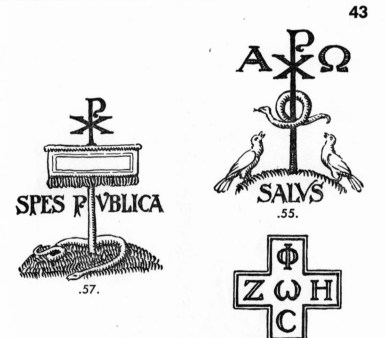

.55.

SPES PVBLICA

.57.

.56.

.54.

.59.

.60.

.61.

.58. The faithful, represented by the sheep, look up to the Savior crucified, the alpha omega on the cross. In the protection of the cross the faithful flourish like palm trees (the palms). From the catacombs.

.59. The faithful, the sheep, look to their Savior, and taking up their crosses follow Him. The idea of this symbol is probably drawn from Matthew (16:24): "If any man will come after Me, let him deny himself, and take up his cross and follow Me." From the catacombs.

.60. The soul of the faithful Christian, the lamb, rests in the shadow of the cross in peace. Peace is symbolized by the dove with the olive branch. From the catacombs.

.61. The Son of God crucified (the Christogram on the cross and the Lamb) offers a place of rest to the faithful (the dove). From the catacombs.

.62. The Lamb of God and the cross stand upon a hill from which flow four streams representing the four Gospels. Through the crucified Savior salvation is brought to mankind represented by the birds. From the catacombs.

44

.62.

.58.

.63. A very beautiful symbolic design taken from the catacombs. The two trees forming a cross offer shade to the birds, who represent the faithful. The fountain of the water of life offers them refreshment.

.64. This represents our Savior in the womb of the Blessed Mother. From the church of Santa Maria Trastevere.

.65. The double candle represents the two natures, divine and human, in our Savior.

.66. Christ, the fish, brings salvation, symbolized by the cross, to the faithful, represented by the bird. The name IHCOUC is fully written. From the catacombs.

.67. The griffin, a mythical creature, half animal and half bird, also represents the two natures in Christ.

.68. The brazen serpent, which by divine command Moses erected in the desert so that the Israelites might look upon it and be healed of the bites of the fiery serpents sent among them by God for their punishment, was a prototype of the Savior. It is often used, however, as a symbol.

.69. The palm tree represents paradise, in which sits Christ, the phoenix. The nimbus is star shaped. An adaptation of a mosaic in the Church of SS. Cosmas and Damian, Rome.

45

.64.

.65.

.66.

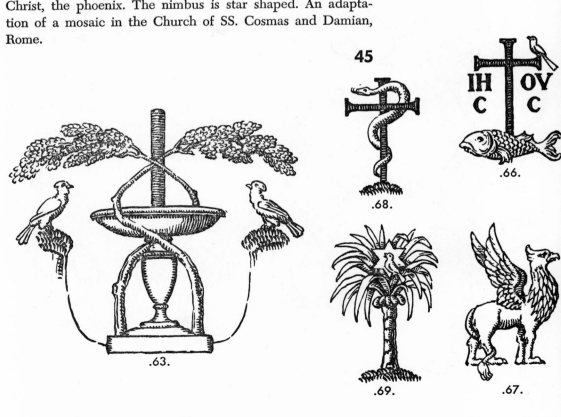

.63.

.68.

.69.

.67.

.70.

.71.

.70. The lamb and the book with seven seals are mentioned by St. John in the Apocalypse. This symbol shows the Lamb of God seated upon the book.

.71. The Lamb of God, Christ, bearing the banner of the resurrection. This is a symbol of the risen Christ.

.72. The Lamb, Christ, carrying the cross, gives His blood for the salvation of man. This is a medieval concept taken from a painting by Martin Schongauer.

.73. and **.75.** Representations of the Sacred Heart of Jesus. A fairly modern concept. See page 38 for restrictions in its use.

.74. This symbol is taken from the catacombs. The lamb is identified as the Savior by the Christogram. The Christogram was used in this way in place of the nimbus to identify figures of our Lord.

.76. The peacock was the ancient pagan symbol of eternity and divinity. It was adopted by the Christians and is used in connection with symbols of the Savior to show His divine character.

.77. The phoenix is a mythical bird, which at the approach of death bursts into flames and arises renewed in strength from its own ashes. It is another symbol of the immortality of Christ.

.78. The instruments of the passion surrounding the representations of the five Sacred Wounds. The whole is a symbol of the Passion of Christ. Taken from a medal designed about A.D. 1670, by Peter Seel, at Salzburg.

46

.72.

.73.

.74.

.75.

.78.

.76.

.77.

47

.79.

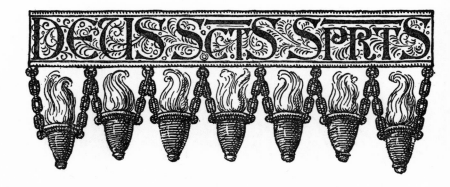

5. THE HOLY SPIRIT

THERE is only one generally recognized symbol for the Holy Spirit, the dove (although there are instances in which the eagle may have this meaning; see baptism), and since the sixth century when it first appeared it has undergone no changes. Upon this, as upon all figures, various styles of art have had their effect; in the age of the early Gothic, it took on very severe forms, while in the eighteenth century it was given a realistic appearance. But these changes were temporary and did not materially affect the symbol. This is true, too, of the different positions in which the dove is depicted. In the early styles it is most often shown descending, or erect with outstretched wings like the heraldic eagle. On the other hand, it may be depicted as flying in a horizontal plane, as is the case especially in the pictures of the annunciation. The nimbus surrounding the dove is always rayed.

During the time of the humanistic movement, and shortly before it, the custom of representing the Holy Spirit in

48

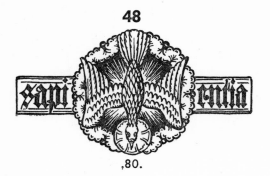

,80.

human form became fairly common. This, however, was prohibited by the Church (Urban VIII, 1623).

There is a further possibility of representing the Holy Spirit, though only indirectly, through the symbols of the seven gifts. The most common symbol is the seven flames, or seven lighted lamps (see chapter headpiece).

.81.

In medieval paintings and stained glass the seven gifts were represented by doves, the dove signifying wisdom predominating in size or in some other manner. In the Middle Ages, too, allegorical female figures were also used for this purpose, each carrying a symbol of one particular gift and bearing a scroll with the Latin name of the gift. These figures bear nimbuses.

The seven gifts of the Holy Spirit are

.82.

.80. Sapientia — Wisdom
.81. Intellectus — Understanding
.82. Consilium — Counsel
.83. Fortitudo — Fortitude
.84. Scientia — Knowledge
.85. Pietas — Piety
.86. Timor — Fear of the Lord

The dove, as has been said, is the one most often seen today, and because of its long use and its scriptural background is eminently suitable, in any connection, as the symbol of the Holy Spirit.

.83.

49

.86.

.85.

.84.

6. THE GOSPELS AND THE EVANGELISTS

WHILE there is a necessary and very close connection between the symbols of the four Gospels and those of the four evangelists, there is nonetheless a clear distinction between them, which must be kept in mind if these symbols are to be used in their true connection. Both groups can be traced to practically contemporary origins in very early times, both being among the most ancient of the truly Christian symbols.

The Gospels themselves were usually represented in the early period by the four rivers of paradise, which also symbolized the four cardinal virtues. They are pictured as flowing from a rock or hill, a reminder that the truth flows from Christ as its source. Sometimes, too, they are shown coming from a large-bodied vase held by a male figure. In some cases

50

the rivers had inscribed upon them their names. These names and the particular Gospel to which each refers are:

Gishon (Gehon or Gihon) — St. Matthew's Gospel
Euphrates — St. Mark's Gospel
Tigris — St. Luke's Gospel
Phison (Pishon or Pison) — St. John's Gospel

These symbols were used in all types of decoration — on small gems as well as in large mosaics.

However, despite their common use in early times, popular knowledge of the four rivers of paradise was gradually lost so that today these symbols of the Gospels are not nearly so often seen as those of the evangelists, which are among the most familiar picture signs of the Church. The winged man, the lion, the ox, and the eagle have been carried on through all the centuries and all periods of art. It is true, however, that the attribution of the single figures to particular evangelists and the reasons for such attribution have not always been the same. Still since about the eleventh century tradition has been fairly constant in holding to one general meaning of the symbols. The explanation which we give here, the one given by most authorities, has evolved during the course of centuries.

The winged man symbolizes St. Matthew, because his Gospel opens with the genealogy of our Divine Savior as man (*Liber generationis Jesu Christi.* Mt. 1:1).

St. Mark is symbolized by the lion, because he writes of John the Baptist whose voice was like the voice of a lion roaring in the wilderness.

The symbol of St. Luke is the ox (or bull), the sacrificial animal, because Luke opens his Gospel with the account of the sacrifice of Zachary. He describes, too, the sacrificial death of our Savior.

The eagle is the symbol of St. John, and fittingly so. John's spirit is like the eagle in its soaring flight to the throne of

51

.88.

.89.

God. If we accept the view of those who sometimes employ the eagle as the symbol of the Holy Spirit, we may consider it in connection with St. John as representing the inspiration of the Holy Spirit in him.

These symbols are used in various ways, but a nimbus and wings are always added to the figures. In medieval styles sometimes the head alone was pictured, a custom which is followed even today, specially in works of medieval character. Sometimes the bust is used; in most cases, however — and this should be the rule — the whole figure is shown. Furthermore there are pictures — though they are seen rarely — which show the symbolical character solely in the head, while the rest of the figure has human form.

As a rule the symbol is completed by the addition of a book or scroll, identifying the symbol. At times even the name of the respective evangelist is inscribed, a feature that detracts much from the symbolical character of the representation. It is true, of course, that no one is inclined or should be expected to solve puzzles in church; but the practice referred to appears somewhat unnecessary as Scripture abounds in quotations that would be suitable to explain the symbols in a dignified way. It would be appropriate, for instance, and sufficient for purposes of identification, to inscribe the first few words of the Gospels on the scrolls of the respective symbolical figures. In this way the purpose of identification would be achieved and the character of the symbol maintained.

.88. From an early gold glass. The four rivers of paradise (the four Gospels) flow from a rock, on which stands a lamb bearing the Christogram on his head. The design is more than a mere symbol of the Gospels. It may even be a

52

.94.

.95.

symbol of the Church. It is mentioned here, however, because it embodies an early symbol of the Gospels.

.89. — .92. The heads of the four symbolical figures with nimbuses and six wings.

.93. A very early design. In the angles formed by the beams of the cross are the four books symbolizing the four Gospels, the whole surrounded by a circle (eternity). The cross in the circle may represent the divine Savior. The whole figure sometimes is included in a square which may symbolize the world. Sometimes the books are so placed that their centers lie in the radius of the circle, they themselves being surrounded by circles which may be nimbuses. Like .88., this does not represent only the Gospels. More likely it is a symbol of the Church, or of our Blessed Savior, of whose sacrificial death on the cross the Gospels tell. A similar design is found in the church of SS. Sylvester and Martin of Tours, at Rome, dating from about A.D. 850.

.94. — .97. The usual symbols of the four evangelists.

53

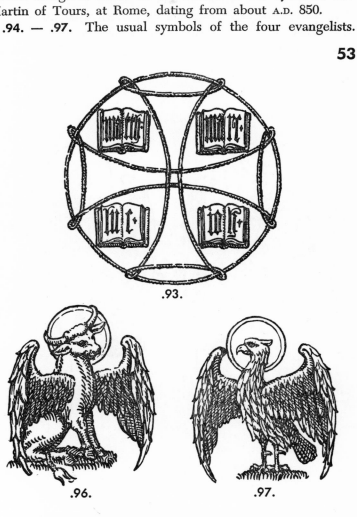

.93.

.96.

.97.

.90.

.91.

.92.

.98.

.98. — .99. The symbolic figures of Matthew and Mark. The bodies, below the heads, are in human form and bear wings. This type of figure is found in the early Renaissance period.

.100. — .101. Half-figures, symbols of the evangelists Luke and John. This concept is taken from medieval German art. In these, as in **.98.** and **.99.**, the figures bear scrolls, with the first words of the Gospels.

.102. This interesting symbol of the evangelists comprises the four symbolical heads in one figure. The design shown here is a free reproduction of an early medieval mosaic found in Monreale (Sicily). It represents a Cherubim with the four symbolical heads, above which hovers the Holy Spirit.

It may be questioned whether this figure was intended originally as a symbol of the evangelists. However, the presence of the dove explains its present attribution. Since we cannot go into the controversy deeply here, we direct the interested reader to Ezechiel 10 for more on this subject.

54

.99.

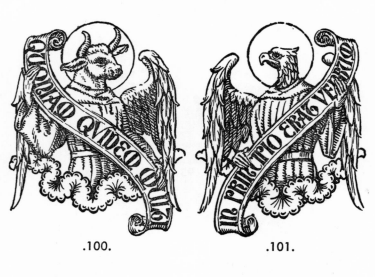

.100.   **.101.**

.102.

7. THE APOSTLES

In THE study or use of the symbols of the twelve Apostles, it is necessary to distinguish between two classes of symbolic devices: those found singly or even in groups which represent individual Apostles, and those which are always found in groups and represent the apostolic college as a whole with our Savior as its head.

Of the first group, namely, those representing individual Apostles, there are no known examples either from very early times or from the Middle Ages. Of the second class, however, several different examples are found in churches of the early times. One of the most ancient of these took the form of the zodiac, in which the various signs represented the Apostles, while in the center instead of the sun, there appeared the head of Christ. The representation of this symbol was forbidden in the year 563, by the Synod of Braga, but because of its decorative possibilities artists continued to use it for many years.

The twelve gems set in the pillar, mentioned in the chapter on the Church, were also used in early times to symbolize the Apostles. The concept may have been drawn from the breastplate worn by the high priest in the Old Testament, which was decorated with twelve precious stones engraved with the names of the twelve tribes of Israel. The Apostles, according to the words of Christ, sit upon twelve seats judging the twelve tribes (cf. pp. 69–70), and hence the idea of using the gems as their symbol.

The symbol most commonly used in this connection in early times consisted of thirteen lambs, the one in the center representing the divine Lamb (cf. Lk. 10:3) and the six on each side representing the Apostles. An example of this symbol is found in the apse of the Church of Santa Maria Pallara, in Rome. The lamb in the center, representing our Blessed Lord, is distinguished by the nimbus and the cross, while the six lambs on each side seem to have come from two houses, one representing Jerusalem, the Old Testament, the other Bethlehem, the New Testament. In later years this symbol has been much used for the decoration of the apse in Romanesque churches. The device has fine decorative possibilities, and can be adapted to various situations. Somewhat similar in concept is the symbol composed of the twelve doves, six on either side of the Savior who is represented by the Christogram enclosed in the circle of eternity.

The Middle Ages contributed two very fine symbols of the Apostles — the twelve stars forming the crown about the head of the Blessed Virgin Mary, and the representation of the heavenly Jerusalem supported by twelve pillars.

The late Middle Ages, probably the heraldry of the sixteenth century, gave rise to an abuse in the use of the attributes of the single Apostles instead of real symbols. The purpose of both heraldry and symbolism is the same, of course, to present practical and historical ideas, but it

57

.103.

.104.

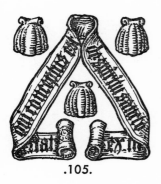

.105.

should be possible to symbolize the single Apostles without resorting to absolutely new material and ideas. And if it is difficult to find proper symbols of the individual Apostles, yet one more medieval idea may be used by applying the articles of the creed to them, as shown below. This notion, of course, has no liturgical or theological basis, but when the attributes of the individual Apostles are shown with these articles of the Creed, the result is a true symbol, and can be approved as such. It must be emphasized once more, that the custom now followed of representing the Apostles by their attributes alone is of late medieval origin.

In the famous church of St. Cecilia de Trastevere, dating from about the year 1200, there is a painting by Cavallini of the Last Judgment, in which the Apostles are shown distinguished, some of them by plain crosses, but only one or the other by the attributes commonly seen today. This may be taken as at least slight evidence that these attributes were not known at that time or at any rate were not in ordinary use.

Following is a list of the articles of the Creed with the Apostles to whom they are attributed:

.103. *Credo in Deum, Patrem omnipotentem* ⎱
I believe in God, the Father Almighty ⎰ · · St. Peter

.104. *Et in Jesum Christum* ⎱
And in Jesus Christ ⎰ · · · · · · St. Andrew

.105. *Qui conceptus est de Spiritu Sancto* ⎱ St. James the
Who was conceived of the Holy Ghost ⎰ Greater

.106. *Passus sub Pontio Pilato* ⎱
Suffered under Pontius Pilate ⎰ · · · · · St. John

.107. *Descendit ad inferos* ⎱
He descended into hell ⎰ · · · · · · St. Philip

.108. *Ascendit ad caelum* ⎱
He ascended into heaven ⎰ · · St. James the Less

.109. *Inde venturus est* ⎱
From thence He shall come again ⎰ · · St. Thomas

58

.106.

.107.

.108.

.110. *Credo in Spiritum Sanctum*
I believe in the Holy Ghost $\Big\}$ . . St. Bartholomew

.111. *Sanctam ecclesiam Catholicam*
In the Holy Catholic Church $\Big\}$ . . St. Matthew

.112. *Remissionem peccatorem*
In the remission of sins $\Big\}$ . . . . . St. Simon

.113. *Carnis resurrectionem*
In the resurrection of the body $\Big\}$ . . . . St. Jude

.114. *Et vitam aeternam*
And in life everlasting $\Big\}$ . . . . St. Matthias

To this list may be added St. Paul, who is distinguished by his attribute the sword and some outstanding passage from his writings. The passage (Gal. 2:20), *"Vivo autem jam non ego, vivit vere in me Christus"* ("And I live, now not I; but Christ liveth in me"), is suggested in **.115.**

While at first glance, then, there seems to be a dearth of symbolic material for the twelve Apostles, the material that does exist, especially the lamb and the dove symbols, offers splendid possibilities to the artist. As symbols they are full of meaning and as decorations much can be done with them.

.115.

59

.109.

.110.

.111.

.112.

.113.

.114.

ECCLESIA SCTA

8. THE CHURCH

THE finest figure of the Church, and the one most often seen in symbol, was given us by the Founder of the Church Himself, who bestowed upon Simon, son of Jona, the new name *Petrus* — rock — calling him the rock upon which He would build His Church. The appropriateness of this figure was recognized at once, and the idea was utilized as early as the third and fourth centuries. In connection with it the early Christians employed the symbols of the Person of Christ, much as we in our day represent St. Peter's in Rome, as a symbol of the Universal Church. The Christogram in the circle or the lamb with the nimbus was depicted standing upon a rock. At times, too, the lamb bore the Christogram upon its head instead of the nimbus. The meaning of the whole symbol was further extended by showing the four rivers of paradise, the four Gospels (cf. p. 51), flowing from the rock. This idea was common in the early ages; it is found on sacred vessels and other objects of the third and

60

fourth centuries, and was used as late as the thirteenth, when Pope Nicholas IV (1288–1292) included it in his decorations of the sanctuary of the Lateran Basilica in one of the most beautifully composed symbols of the Church that still remain to us (see **.118.**).

Another symbol of the Church fairly common in early times is that of Moses striking the rock. This is found in gold paintings on glasses* which were undoubtedly liturgical vessels. This symbol is referred by some archaeologists to the Holy Eucharist and by others to the sacrament of baptism. It is important to note, however, that some of the early examples of this symbol carry an inscription which is, without doubt, the word *Petrus*, and in view of this fact, it is difficult to see any other application than to the Church. Peter, the head of the Church on earth, causes the spiritual water to flow as Moses did the real water, by striking the rock in the desert. This concept is strengthened by 1 Cor. 10:4, where the Apostle, in speaking of the Israelites, says: "And they drank of the spiritual rock that followed them, and the rock was Christ."

What is said in the chapter on the sacraments concerning the difficulty of attributing a specific meaning to certain symbols applies to another early symbol, the four open books placed in the angles formed by the beams of a cross. A beautiful example of this device is found in the church of SS. Sylvester and Martin of Tours in Rome (about A.D. 850), and although most authors consider it as a figure of the Gospels, under which aspect we have treated it on page 53, it may very well refer to the Church.

Paul, in his first letter to Timothy (3:15) calls "the Church of the living God, the pillar and ground of truth." This idea

---

*Commonly called gold glass. Glassware ornamented with designs engraved on gold foil, attached to the glass and then protected by a thin film of glass.

was often represented in the early days and in many different ways: it was shown in large frescoes as well as on small ring stones. Sometimes the pillar was shown standing on a rock; sometimes it was surmounted by the lamb or by the Christogram. At times, too, it was an ornate pillar, decorated with twelve precious stones to symbolize the twelve Apostles (or one stone might be missing — a figure of Judas). But however represented, the pillar is not rare among the early symbols, and there is little doubt but that to the first Christians it was a symbol — and a most appropriate one — of the Church Universal.

A very beautiful painting employing this motif is found in the catacomb of St. Callixtus, and shown on page 82. The Church is symbolized by the pillar on which stands a vessel containing blood: on the right, representing the faithful, there is a lamb gazing upon the vessel; on the left there is a second lamb with its face turned away from the pillar, symbolizing the Jews.

The first Christians favored one other symbol of the Church, especially for the decoration of the tombs in the catacombs. This symbol, the ship, is common even today as the figure of the bark of Peter, which carries the faithful Christian across the wild sea of life to the port of eternal joy, heaven.

There are other early symbols which may refer to the Church but which are rarely seen in that connection. The stags drinking from the spring, for example, mentioned in the section on baptism, page 74, could be used for this purpose, for the Church is the channel from which the faithful may drink the waters of eternal life. However, it is less confusing to avoid the use of symbols that have several applications, particularly when there are, as in this case, those which apply directly.

Besides the simple symbols of the Church, there are others

62

which symbolize it in contrast to the synagogue, the new Jerusalem to the old Jerusalem, the New Testament to the Old Testament. These signs referring to the antithesis between the Church and Judaism, the New Testament and the Old Testament, the new Jerusalem and the old, are found especially since the Middle Ages.

It was one of the delights of medieval artists to personify abstract ideas. This penchant was carried into sacred art, and in accord with it the Church was represented by a beautiful and stately virgin, crowned and bearing a cruciform staff and a chalice, and the Synagogue by a blindfolded female figure. This latter figure is sometimes shown with a crown slipping from its head, and the tables of the law falling from the hands. Famous examples of such figures are found in the Cathedral of Strassburg in Alsace, and at Bamberg in Bavaria. Besides their symbolic value these particular statues bear witness to the perfection of medieval sculpture.

The Middle Ages gave us other examples of this contrast — the sun and moon, for instance; the sun, of course, representing the Church. Later it was shown by the single candle on the three-legged candlestick and the seven-branched candlestick. The Christogram and the Hebrew characters of the name *Jaweh* likewise present this contrast.

Recent centuries have given us a few outstanding symbols of the Church. Some of them are: the ark and rainbow, the sign of God's covenant with man; the beehive, whose wonderful organization is a figure of the organization of the Church, and the constant renewal of whose queen is a symbol of the unbroken succession of popes. These, though good, are somewhat too involved to enjoy much favor.

The headpiece of this chapter, finally, while it is an allegorical rather than a symbolical representation, is a beautiful figure of the Church. It is taken from a fourth-century sculpture found in Dalmatia. In this particular example the

63

ship is shown with Christ as the steersman, but there are others known in which this position is occupied by a figure of Peter. These last are of early date also, and are among the most authentic proofs that Peter was considered from the very first head of the Church on earth.

Because the contrast between the old and the new dispensations is important for purposes of symbolization, it has been thought well to add two tables containing symbols taken from the Old Testament. The symbols of the twelve tribes of Israel will be useful for contrast with the symbols of the twelve Apostles. The designs shown here have behind them a long tradition, and are based by some on the forty-ninth chapter of Genesis and the thirty-third of Deuteronomy. The designs bear the Hebrew script although it might be preferable to substitute the Latin or even the English.

.116. This symbol of the Church is found on an early gold glass (see note, p. 61). It represents St. Peter, like Moses, striking the rock from which flows the water. The rock itself symbolizes the Church, while the stream is a figure of the life-giving stream of grace which flows from the Church. This symbol is extremely important because of the unequivocal meaning given it by the inscription *Petrus*.

.117. The pillar represents the Church and the twelve gems which ornament it are the twelve Apostles. From the capital grow a number of palms, the palms of eternal life. Over them, standing upon a rainbow which may refer to the rainbow given Noe as a sign of the covenant, or to the rainbow mentioned in the Apocalypse (4:3) as being "round about the throne of God," is a lamb identified as Christ by the Christogram and the circle of infinity. The birds and lambs represent the faithful, who look to the Church as the pillar and source of salvation.

The figure is taken from a gem coming from the time of the catacombs.

64

PETRVS

.116.

.117.

65

JORDANES

.118.

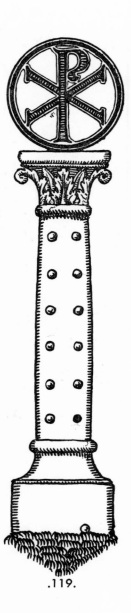

.119.

.118. This symbol forms the centerpiece of the decoration of the apse in the Lateran Basilica at Rome. It is a beautiful and complete symbol of the Church.

From the Holy Spirit, symbolized by the dove, water flows through Christ, the cross, into the Church, the rock. Out of the rock come the rivers of salvation, from which drink the faithful, symbolized by the lambs and stags.

Beneath the rock is a symbol of paradise, the reward of the faithful, in which are a number of souls guarded by an angel.

.119. The Church is symbolized by the pillar surmounted by the Christogram representing Christ. The pillar is ornamented with eleven jewels, the eleven Apostles. The jewel which has fallen to the ground represents the traitor Judas.

.120. The Church, under the protection of Christ, brings the reward of heaven, the wreath, to the faithful.

.121. Under His holy name, Christ, the fish (see Chapter 4, God the Son), carries the Church through the waves of trouble and error.

.122. The faithful, symbolized by the dove, ride the ship, the Church, under the protection of Christ. They receive the heavenly reward, the palms.

.123. Under the guidance of the cross, Christ, the ship, symbolizing the Church, sails safely into port.

.124. A more modern symbol of the Church. The beehive is an example of orderly life and organization, and hence represents the life and organization of the Church.

.125. The rainbow and the ark both refer to the covenant

67

.120.

.121.

.122.

.123.

.124.

.125.

made by God with Noe. The whole is a symbol of the Church, the new covenant.

.126. A late realistic symbol. St. Peter's standing upon the rock, represents the Universal Church. This symbol is found often during the past centuries.

.127. The Star of David with the inscription *Jaweh* in Hebrew characters. The star represents the power of *Jaweh* which reaches to all corners of the earth.

68

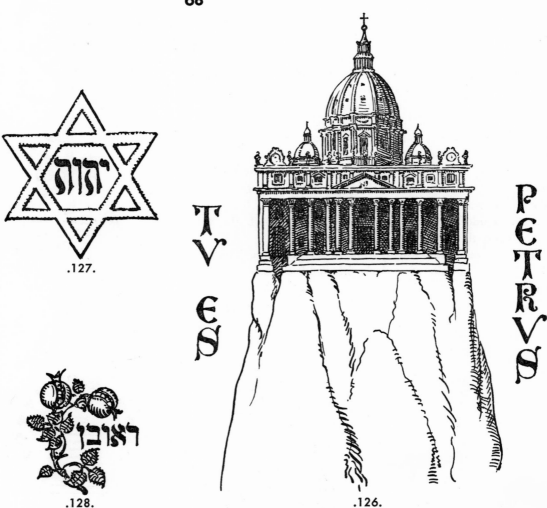

.127.

.128.

.126.

.128. The pomegranate, symbol of the tribe of Ruben.

.129. The fortress is the symbol of the tribe of Simeon because of the fact that the father of the tribe took the fortress of Sichem and slew the inhabitants (Gen. 34).

.130. Symbol of the tribe of Levi, the priestly tribe. This represents the breastplate worn by the high priest, bearing the twelve precious stones which had engraved upon them the names of the twelve tribes.

.131. The lion of Juda. This is derived from the words of Genesis (49:9): "Juda is a lion's whelp . . . thou hast couched as a lion. . . ."

.132. The tribe of Isaachar was engaged in land trade. Hence the camel, the common beast of burden in the orient, is the symbol of this tribe.

.133. The tribe of Zabulon was engaged in sea trade. The ship is its symbol. "Zabulon shall dwell on the sea shore, and in the road of ships" (Gen. 49:13).

.134. The seven-branched candlestick was one of the prominent fittings of the temple (Exod. 25). It is taken as a symbol of the Old Testament.

.135. The tables of the law upon which the Lord inscribed the ten commandments given to Moses are a symbol of the Old Testament. They are indicated here by the Hebrew numbers. The first tablet contains the commandments regulating man's relation to God: the second the commandments referring to his relation with men.

69

.129.

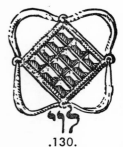

.130.

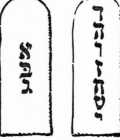

.131.

.132.

.133.

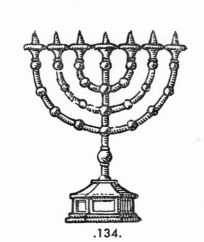

.134.

.135.

.136.

.137.

.136. The serpent is the symbol of the tribe of Dan. "Let Dan be a snake in the way, a serpent in the path" (Gen. 49:17).

.137. The tribe of Gad. The tents probably refer to the promise made by the tribe to Moses that the fighting men would not dwell in houses until Chanaan had been subdued (Num. 32).

.138. Nephthali, the doe. Scripture says "Nephthali, a hart let loose" (Gen. 49:21).

.139. The tribe of Aser is symbolized by the breadfruit tree. Genesis (49:20) says: "Aser, his bread shall be fat, and he shall yield dainties to kings."

.140. The symbols of the tribe of Joseph, the bull and the unicorn, are in reality the symbols of his sons Manasses and Ephraim (Deut. 33:17).

.141. The tribe of Benjamin has for its sign the wolf. "Benjamin is a ravenous wolf" (Gen. 49:27).

70

.138.

.139.

.140.

.141.

9. THE SACRAMENTS

REPRESENTATION of the seven sacraments in a connected series of symbols demands some considerable artistic resourcefulness and liturgical feeling. This is owing to the variety of sources from which the symbols come and to their consequent difference of atmosphere and liturgical significance. It is quite probable that all seven of the sacraments were represented by symbols as early as the times of the catacombs, but today many, if not most of these early symbols are unknown, and this for two reasons. First, it must be remembered that only a small part of the symbolic treasures of the catacombs still exists today; time and long periods of neglect have done their work of destruction. Second, with many of those that do still exist, there is the difficulty of ascertaining exactly the significance originally given to them. Archaeologists attribute a general meaning to many of the symbols that certainly had a very specific application for the

71

ancients. For instance, the picture of the two small fishes approaching the anchor probably represents the desire of the faithful for the protection and salvation held out to them by the cross; but this symbol might just as truly represent the desire of two persons to be united under the cross, and thus symbolize in a beautiful manner the sacrament of matrimony. Hence, there must be a certain hesitancy about attributing any unquestionable meaning to these symbols, and the fact is that the most eminent of the archaeologists, such as Rossi, Garrucci, Marucchi, and Wilpert — who first brought to light the great treasure house of early symbols, the catacombs — do not always explain them in the same way.

In the face of this lack of early and specific symbols, many new ones have been devised during the past centuries which, compared with the earlier ones that do exist, are wanting in both spiritual beauty and meaning. The artist, then, who wishes to represent the seven sacraments in a series is faced with a very real problem. A partial solution for this may be found in a close study of the ritual and the liturgy of the sacraments, for from such a study he may gain some ideas which he can utilize to modify and give specific meaning to already existing symbols and thus create something worth while.

As indicated in Chapter I, the decorations and symbols of a church or its parts should combine to form a complete, organic picture, deriving as far as possible from the same period and having the same underlying philosophy. For example, if there are seven windows, each to carry a symbol of one of the sacraments, it is surely incongruous to represent on one of them baptism by a picture of a baptismal font and on another the Holy Eucharist by the fish and the basket of bread. The latter is one of the oldest and most beautiful of symbols found in the art of the catacombs, and to couple it with the former, a modern and not too significant

72

symbol, argues a certain lack of ingenuity and sense of artistic fitness. True, no one will mistake the meaning of the
baptismal font, but the essential idea of any sacrament is not
the liturgical instrument used in its administration, but the
supernatural grace conferred by it, and it is this that should
form the basis of the symbol.

The representation of single sacraments, apart from a
series, naturally presents fewer difficulties, although even
here care must be taken to guard against thoughtlessness.
And this book, though it has for its purpose to supply actual
material for decoration, would be incomplete did it not point
out some of the more common mistakes in this sphere. Now,
there are certainly more appropriate and thought-provoking
symbols to be had in decorating a baptismal chapel than
the aforementioned picture of the baptismal font. Likewise,
it is only poverty of ideas or carelessness that will decorate,
as is so commonly done, an antependium with chalice and
host surrounded by wheat and grapes. This symbol is over-
worked to say the least; but more than that, on an antependium it is merely a weak figure of What is really present on
the altar itself. Finally, it is the height of incongruity to
engrave on the sacred vessels used in the administration of
extreme unction, the oil stocks as a symbol of the sacrament.
It is, in other words, rather too much to ornament an instrument with a picture of itself.

The whole field of sacramental symbols, finally, affords a
splendid opportunity for the judicious use of scriptural quotations, and for applying them to symbols that we already
have, some of which date from the times of the catacombs,
thus enlarging and deepening their meaning.

BAPTISM

There are only a few authentic symbols which refer exclusively to the sacrament of baptism, although some very fine accommodations of other symbols can be made. The symbolism of this sacrament is, for instance, closely connected with that of the Holy Spirit and the Holy Trinity, and since baptism is the primary means of receiving the Holy Spirit a most natural symbol of the sacrament is the dove (see Acts 8:18). Then there is the further possibility of using in this connection the other signs of the Holy Spirit, the seven rays or seven flames.

Other appropriate symbols, and useful for the decoration of baptismal chapels or fonts, are the stags seeking the fountain of living water (Ps. 41:2) or the doves drinking from the fountain. These may refer as well to the Holy Eucharist, but there is nothing against their being used in connection with baptism. Both of them are found in frescoes in the catacombs, and come from as early as A.D. 300. They are found, too, in the mausoleum of Galla Placidia, in Rome, dating about A.D. 450.

There is one other symbol, of somewhat the same general nature, found on a carved ring-stone of Arnulf, the Bishop of Metz in Lorraine, and coming from the seventh century, which may be considered as a sign of baptism although not exclusively. It portrays two fish approaching from either side a basket which already holds a third fish. Its meaning is quite plain (see fish).

Another symbol mentioned by most books on this subject, but seldom seen today is the stag vomiting the poison which has been injected into it by a serpent. Obviously, this would be repulsive to modern tastes, but it really has a depth of meaning. It signifies that baptism frees the soul of the poison

74

of sin, and the idea is drawn from the so-called *Physiologus,* a Christian work of the third century, which described animals, real and imaginary, and gave to them an allegorical meaning (see *Catholic Encyclopedia,* Vol. XII).

In the floor of the baptistry in Capua there is a beautiful symbol which undoubtedly refers to the sacrament of baptism. It is a mosaic representing an eagle in flight, carrying a fish in its talons. The fish, of course, represents the soul which has taken on the character of Christ through baptism and is carried by the eagle to great heights. In another explanation, the eagle is taken to represent the Holy Spirit, in which case the meaning of the whole symbol would be that the soul represented by the fish, with the aid of the Holy Spirit, the eagle, is carried to heaven.

There is another sign, taken today almost exclusively as a sign of the Trinity, which in early times certainly referred to baptism. In fact, the use of this symbol in this connection seems to be much older than the earliest example of it known to us. This is the three fishes arranged in the form of a triangle and treated in this work in the chapter on the Most Holy Trinity (cf. p. 24). The device appears first on a copper vessel from the island of Seeland, in the Baltic Sea, which was possibly used in the administration of the sacrament of baptism during medieval times. It must be emphasized, however, that the symbol itself is distinctly not medieval in concept, but comes from an earlier period in the Christian era. It does, of course, refer to the Trinity in a special way, but it symbolizes baptism also because baptism is administered in the name of the Holy Trinity (see Mt. 28:19). The device is eminently suitable for the decoration of liturgical objects used in the administration of the sacrament, although it will hardly do in large-scale decorations; for these the stags and doves, mentioned earlier, provide sufficient material.

The two modern symbols often seen are neither of them

75

so full of meaning or so valuable from the decorative stand-point as the ancient ones. The baptismal font indeed has some meaning: It is intimately connected with the conferring of the sacrament, and as a sign of his power to baptize it is presented to a pastor at his formal installation by the bishop. But it is no traditional symbol, and if used at all, it should be restricted to small-scale graphic work, and not used for decoration in a church where, it may be presumed, there is already a font, the reality from which the symbol is taken.

The other modern symbol is the picture of the hand pouring water from a shell. Strictly speaking, this is not a symbol but only a detail taken from a complete picture. There may be, nevertheless, some justification for it if the dove is shown in connection with it. Incidentally, the other sacraments could be represented by a similar device, and with as much reason; for instance, the Holy Eucharist might be symbolized by a hand holding a host. However, the effect of a whole series of such representations might be somewhat disquieting.

CONFIRMATION

The early ages have yielded but one symbol that has behind it the force of constant tradition as being applied to the sacrament of confirmation, and that one, as in the case of baptism, is an accommodated symbol — the dove of the Holy Spirit. When used in reference to confirmation, however, it should be accompanied by the seven flames, to signify the seven gifts of the Holy Spirit conferred by the sacrament. Or the dove may carry the olive branch. These two additions will aid the artist against duplication when representing the sacraments in a series.

THE HOLY EUCHARIST

The sacrament of the Savior's Body and Blood, like the Person of our divine Lord itself, was from the first the center of a most beautiful growth of symbols. In fact, it is somewhat difficult to tell in a particular instance whether a symbol refers to one or the other, for nearly all the symbols of the Savior refer, at least in a sense, to the Blessed Eucharist and vice versa.

The catacombs are veritable treasuries of eucharistic symbols, and naturally so. For these vast underground galleries were not merely burial places for the dead but in certain circumstances places of assembly for the living. Here the Christians came together, sometimes under the guise of burial societies, to celebrate their mysteries — here they were comparatively safe from their fierce persecutors, for even to the pagans places of burial were sacred, and burial societies were protected by Roman law.

Now, in order to participate more really in the celebration of the sublime mysteries, the first Christians received Holy Communion whenever they attended. Mass and the reception of the Holy Eucharist were inseparable for these early Martyrs — and hence it is not strange that the places where this divine sacrifice was offered were decorated with symbols of it. It is important for the understanding of some of these symbols, however, to know that the manner of receiving Holy Communion was different in those early times from what it is today; forms and accidental emphasis change in the Church as elsewhere, even though basic doctrines remain the same. In the early days, then, the Sacred Species was placed by the priest upon the right palm of the communicant who then consumed it. Besides this, while it might be possible to celebrate Mass only occasionally, the early be-

77

lievers sought to be united with Christ at all times by Holy Communion. Hence, the Eucharist was kept in their homes, where they communicated themselves.* It was carried from the place of sacrifice in wicker baskets, as may be seen from the words of St. Jerome (*Epis. ad Rusticum*), "No one is more happy than he who carries the Body and Blood in a basket" (*canistrum*, i.e., reed or willow basket).

In this connection there is an early notice which is not directly pertinent here but which shows that the early days were not so far different from our own; it is that the preachers were wont to speak of the shamelessness of Christians attending the theater, "as they return from the Sacrifice, carrying the Eucharist, as is customary."

Applying this idea, one theme among the mural decorations of the catacombs is that of the fish bearing on its back a basket of loaves, with a glass vessel of wine appearing through the meshes of the basket. The fish, of course, represents Christ; the loaves, His Body; and the wine, His Blood; the whole signifying that Christ Himself brings the Eucharist to the faithful. A beautiful example of this symbol is found in the Crypt of Lucina, in the Catacomb of St. Callixtus, and dates from the second century.

Sometimes there are shown five loaves toward which two fishes are swimming, the numbers five and two referring to the miracle of the loaves and fishes narrated in John 6. Other symbols, referring specifically to the desire of the faithful for the grace of the Eucharist are the birds eating grapes or drinking from a fountain, and the stags approaching the spring.

The Middle Ages gave us one beautiful symbol of the Holy Eucharist, the pelican which, according to popular legend, opens its breast to feed its young upon its blood. This is a

---

* For full explanation of this, see *Christian Life and Worship*, by Gerald Ellard, S.J.

touching symbol of Christ who feeds mankind in the Sacrament of His Body and Blood.

These are only some of the beautiful symbols of the Blessed Sacrament. Others are shown on pages 82–85.

PENANCE

Penance is often symbolized by the keys, the symbol of the power to bind and loose given to Peter by our Savior (Mt. 16:19) and ordinarily exercised through the sacrament of penance. Sometimes, too, the scourge is used to represent this sacrament although its application is not entirely apt, for penance liberates the soul from the scourge of sin. It would seem, then, to be more properly the symbol of eternal punishment.

The one early symbol that we have, however, which beyond doubt refers to this sacrament, offers a happy solution of this problem. It is found in a painting in the Church of SS. Peter and Marcellinus in Rome, and pictures an orans (a female figure with arms outstretched in prayer, see note on page 87) at whose side there is a scourge with a single lash disconnected as though falling away. It signifies that the soul has been freed from the power of the scourge through the grace of absolution. It was probably meant to emphasize against the Montanists and Novations the teaching of the Church that all sins, without exception, can be forgiven through the sacrament of penance. However this may be, there is gained from it a very fine symbol of the sacrament — the scourge with one or more lashes parted from the stock.

EXTREME UNCTION

The most commonly used symbol of this sacrament, the lighted candles, the hour glass with sands almost run out, and the oil stock, is the result of sheer necessity for a symbol. It is poor, and it might be better to use the device so often shown on the tombs in the catacombs, the dove with the olive branch of peace (see **.60.**). This latter is a splendid symbol of the effects of the sacrament, but there is no historical proof that when first used it was actually applied to extreme unction.

HOLY ORDERS

There is also no historical proof for the ancient use of our symbols for the sacrament of holy orders. The chalice, showing the power of sacrifice; the book, the teaching power; and the stole, the pastoral power, are often seen. Of these the chalice alone has been used for any considerable length of time, and that only since the late Middle Ages, when it appeared often on the tombstones of priests.

MATRIMONY

The device most commonly applied to the sacrament of matrimony is the joined hands, which takes its symbolic meaning from 1 Cor. 7:4: "The wife hath not power of her own body, but the husband. And in like manner the husband hath not power of his own body, but the wife." The sacramental character is brought out by the stole which is sometimes shown laid across the hands and also by the monogram of Jesus placed above them.

Matrimony may also be symbolized by the device mentioned earlier in this chapter, the two fishes approaching the anchor, and signifying the desire of union under the cross. There is no proof, however, that it was given this meaning in early times.

There is one more symbol possible — the crown. This takes its meaning from the early custom of employing the crown in the wedding ceremony, a custom that still survives in some places. Among the orthodox believers in Russia, for example, a great crown is held over the bridal couple during the marriage ceremony; in the Black Forest, and in Hungary the bride wears a crown of tinsel ornamented with glass jewels. The wreath commonly worn by brides, in some parts of the Old World called bride's crown, may be a survival of this custom.

HEADPIECE

The rainbow, in the old dispensation, was a sign of God's covenant with men. It is most fittingly a type of the New Covenant made by Christ and carried out through the medium of the sacraments. The seven colors of the rainbow are a symbol of the seven sacraments.

.142.

BAPTISM

.142. The dove of the Holy Spirit who is given to the soul in baptism. The seven flames symbolize His seven gifts. However, when used as a symbol of baptism, the dove is usually, though not necessarily, shown without the flames.

.143. This device is taken from a ring stone of Arnulf, Bishop of Metz. It may well have reference to the words of Christ to His Apostles: "Come ye after Me, and I will make

.143.

81

.144.

you to be fishers of men" (Mt. 4:19). In this figure the one fish is held in the basket while the other two approach.

.144. This device is taken from a mosaic in the floor of the baptistry at Capua. The soul which has taken on the character of Christ, indicated by the fish, is being taken by the Holy Spirit, the eagle, to heaven.

CONFIRMATION

.142. The dove of the Holy Spirit, with the seven flames signifying the seven gifts which are conferred in the sacrament of confirmation.

HOLY EUCHARIST

.145.

.145. This symbol, employing the fish motif, portrays the faithful (the fish) eating the bread of life.

.146. This symbol, taken from a fresco in the catacombs, employs several different symbolic elements. The Holy Eucharist, the vase containing blood, stands atop a pillar which represents the Church. The lamb at the right represents the faithful yearning after the blood of the Redeemer. The lamb at the left, turned away from the pillar, represents the Jews who would not accept this marvelous gift but turned away from it.

.147. This is a later adaptation of the stag and fountain symbol. The stag, symbolizing the faithful, thirsts for the cooling waters, the Holy Eucharist, symbolized by the chalice.

.148. This symbol, taken from a seventh-century lamp, represents the Holy Eucharist under both species. The fish symbolizes the Sacred Body, and the vase contains the Sacred Blood.

82

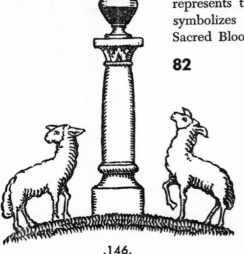

.146.

.147.

.148.

.149. The number of fish and breads in this symbol are interesting and bring to mind the miracle of the multiplication of loaves and fishes narrated by St. Matthew (14:13–21). It is taken from a ring stone of the third or fourth century and represents the faithful hungering after the bread of life.

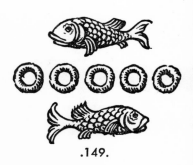

.149.

.150. The outstanding ancient symbol of the Holy Eucharist. It is taken from the crypt of St. Lucina, in the Catacomb of St. Callixtus. Christ, the fish, Himself brings to the faithful His Body and Blood, symbolized by the basket containing the bread and wine. In all symbols of this kind the fish is shown with its head *above the water*. This fact most probably had some symbolic meaning although that meaning has been lost through the ages. (For fuller explanation see pages 36 and 77.)

.151. From its form, this symbol may well have served at one time as a *crux dissimulata* (cf. p. 30). It represents, of course, the faithful approaching the bread of life. It is taken from a marble relief in a baptistery at Carthage.

.152. This symbol, taken from an ancient ring stone, represents the faithful hungering for the bread of life.

83

.151.

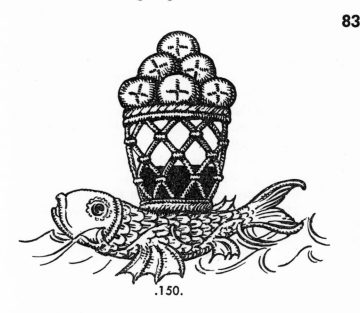

.150.

.152.

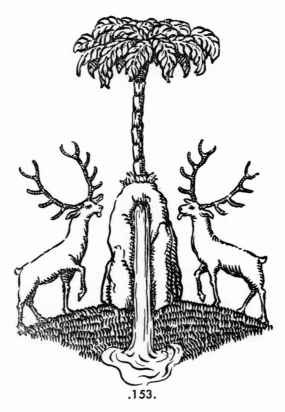

.153.

.153. The idea of the stags and the fountain, probably drawn from Ps. 41:2, was much favored in early times for symbolic uses. The figure shown here is an adaptation of a symbol found in the mausoleum of Galla Placidia, and used often in later times. The stags symbolize the faithful who thirst after the living water which is figured flowing from the rock. The rock itself is a symbol of Christ or of the Church, while the palm growing from it suggests the heavenly reward given to those who are nourished on the Blood of Christ.

.154. The pelican as a symbol of Christ was probably not used before the thirteenth century. Its symbolic meaning is derived from the *Physiologus* (see p. 75), which told of the pelican drawing the blood from its own breast to feed its young. It is, however, a splendid symbol of the Blessed Sacrament in which Christ feeds men on His Most Precious Blood. Thomas Aquinas uses the figure in his beautiful Eucharistic hymn the *Adoro Te Devote:*

> *Pie Pelicane, Jesu Domine,*
> *Me immundum munda Tuo sanguine.*

.154.

.155. This is probably the best-known symbol today. The sheaf of wheat refers to the Blessed Sacrament. The grain is heavy, reminding us of the rich blessings which flow from the Sacrament.

.156. This bird-and-grape motif is often found on sarcophagi dating from the ancient classic times. The faithful are symbolized by the birds who are eating the grapes — the Blood of Christ.

.157. A modern conventional symbol of the Eucharist.

.155.

PENANCE

.158. The scourge as a symbol of penance dates from the fourth century. This figure shows two of the lashes detached from the scourge, a clear symbol of sins already forgiven.

.159. In St. Matthew's Gospel (16:19) we read: "And I will give to thee the keys of the kingdom of heaven. And whatsoever thou shalt bind upon earth it shall be bound also in heaven; and whatsoever thou shalt loose on earth it shall be loosed also in heaven." The keys, then, are a most apt symbol of the sacrament of the forgiveness of sins. Modern art combines them with the scourge — the symbol of punishment or penance.

.156.

85

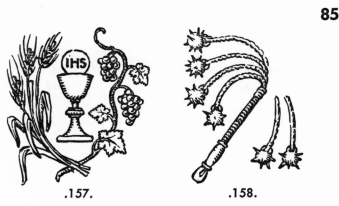

.157.

.158.

.159.

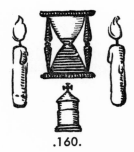

EXTREME UNCTION

.160. This symbol is often used today but it actually has little to recommend it. For other suggestions see Extreme Unction, page 80.

.160.

HOLY ORDERS

.161. This modern arrangement of several symbolic elements is often used as a symbol of the sacrament of holy orders. The chalice and host represent the sacrificial character of the priesthood; the book is a sign of the teaching power; the stole symbolizes the pastoral power.

MATRIMONY

.162. The use of the rings to symbolize the sacrament of matrimony is of recent origin. This device symbolizes the joining of man and woman in an unending union, under the protection of Christ, who is symbolized by the monogram.

.163. This is a more concrete symbol. The joined hands are bound together by the stole representing the sacrament, under the protection of Christ, the monogram.

86

.161.

.162.

.163.

10. THE BLESSED VIRGIN MARY

CONSIDERING the universality of the cult of the Blessed Virgin Mary, it is surprising to note that there are no recognized early symbols of the Mother of God. That is not to say that there were no such symbols in the early ages, but only that they are not recognized as such today. There are in the catacombs many *pictures* of the Blessed Virgin; in some of them she is carrying the divine Child, and in others she is represented in the well-known figure of the orans.* On some of the pictures is the inscription ΜΑΡΙΑ ΜΗΤΗΡ ΘΕΟΥ (*Maria Meter theou*) — "Mary the Mother of God," and on others the words ΑΕΙ ΠΑΡΘΕΝΟC — "ever Virgin" or Η ΠΗΓΗ (*He Pege*) — "the fountain." These figures are all interesting from the archaeological and theological points of view, but they are

---

*A female figure with extended arms. A familiar subject in the art of the Catacombs. Cf. *Catholic Encyclopedia*, Vol. VI, article "Orans."

87

of little value for modern decorative purposes. They presuppose too much knowledge of liturgical archaeology and the tradition necessary for their understanding has long since been lost.

Two of the above-mentioned pictures are shown here — **.166.** and **.167.** — not as a suggestion that they be used but merely for the sake of completeness and to convey some idea of the depth and beauty of early art.

The headpiece of this chapter shows the Blessed Virgin with outstretched arms in the attitude of prayer (orans). The manner of representing the Child Jesus symbolizes His presence within the womb of His Virgin Mother. This picture form is called the *Maria Platytera;* the monogram, ΑΓΙΑ ΜΑΡΙΑ (*Hagia Maria*) — "Holy Mary," does not appear on the original but is taken from another picture of about the same time — A.D. 750. The design is adapted from a sculpture in the Church of Santa Maria Mater Domini, Venice.

If the material from early times seems scant, the Middle Ages gave us a corresponding abundance. Medieval artists used as the basis for symbolic designs the ideas which later on (about A.D. 1500) were collected as invocations in the *Litany of Loreto* while the Canticle of Canticles provided other inspirations.

The invocations of the litany are especially suitable for symbolic representation, and to present these ideas in simple designs is not difficult and is capable of much artistic development. Besides, the faithful are already familiar with the ideas of the litany and will understand and appreciate fully their representation.

Artists of the seventeenth and eighteenth centuries, realizing the possibilities of these designs, often enriched their meaning with quotations from Sacred Scripture. Designs based upon the litany and taken largely from the *Laure-*

88

tanische Litanei by F. X. Dorn (Augsburg, 1757) are shown in **.186.** and following. The litany is also included here, with an appropriate Scripture quotation for each invocation.

Kyrie eleison
Lord, have mercy

Christe eleison
Christ, have mercy

Kyrie eleison
Lord, have mercy

Christe, audi nos
Christ, hear us

Christe, exaudi nos
Christ, graciously hear us
Pater de Coelis Deus
God, the Father of heaven
Fili Redemptor mundi Deus
God the Son, Redeemer of
the world.
Spiritus Sancte Deus
God, the Holy Ghost

Sancta Trinitas Unus Deus
Holy Trinity, One God
Sancta Maria
Holy Mary

(Et) Laudis ejus plena est terra (Hab. 3:3).
"And the earth is full of His praise."
Dixitque ei: Petitionem unam parvulam deprecor a te, ne confundas faciem meam. Et dixit ei Rex; Pete Mater mea: neque enim fas est, ut avertam faciem tuam (3 Kings 2:20).
"And she said to him: I desire one small petition of thee, do not put me to confusion. And the king said to her: my mother, ask: for I must not turn away thy face."
Adeamus ergo cum fiducia ad thronum gratiae, ut misericordiam consequamur (Hebr. 4:16).
"Let us go, therefore, with confidence to the throne of grace; that we may obtain mercy."
Ego exaudiam de coelo, et propitius ero . . . (2 Par. 7:14).
"(Then) will I hear from heaven, and will be merciful. . . ."
Exaudivit me Dominus (Deut. 9:19).
"The Lord heard me."
Cujus es Filia? indica mihi (Gen. 24:23).
"Whose daughter art thou? tell me."
Scio, enim quod Redemptor meus vivit (Job. 19:25).
"For I know that my Redeemer liveth."
Una est Columba mea, perfecta mea, una est Matris suae, Electa genitrici suae (Cant. 6:8).
"One is my dove, my perfect one . . . the only one of her mother, the chosen of her that bore her."
Hi tres unum sunt (1 Jn. 5:7).
"These three are One."
Benedictus Dominus, qui . . . hodie Nomen tuum ita magnificavit, ut non recedat laus tua de ore hominum (Judith 13:24, 25).
"Blessed be the Lord who . . . hath so

89

Sancta Dei genitrix
Holy Mother of God

Sancta virgo virginum
Holy Virgin of Virgins

Mater Christi
Mother of Christ

Mater divinae gratiae
Mother of divine grace

Mater purissima
Mother most pure

Mater castissima
Mother most chaste

Mater inviolata
Mother inviolate

Mater intemerata
Mother undefiled

Mater amabilis
Mother most amiable

Mater admirabilis
Mother most admirable
Mater creatoris
Mother of our Creator

Mater salvatoris
Mother of our Redeemer

magnified thy name this day that thy praise shall not depart out of the mouth of men."
Peperit Filium suum primogenitum (Lk. 2:7).
"She brought forth her first-born Son."
Viderunt eam Filiae, et beatissimam praedicaverunt (Cant. 6:8).
"The daughters saw her, and declared her most blessed."
Te in utero novem mensibus portavi, et lac dedi . . . et alui (2 Mach. 7:27).
"I bore thee nine months in my womb, and gave thee suck . . . and nourished thee."
Adeamus . . . ad thronum gratiae (Hebr. 4:16).
"Let us go . . . to the throne of grace."
Deus mundavit, tu commune ne dixeris (Acts 11:9).
"God hath made clean, do not thou call common."
O quam pulchra est casta generatio (Wisd. 4:1).
"O how beautiful is the chaste generation."
Eo quod castitatem amaveris . . . ideo eris benedicta in aeternum (Judith 15:11).
"Because thou hast loved chastity . . . therefore thou shalt be blessed forever."
Portae inferi non praevalebunt adversus eam (Mt. 16:18).
"The gates of hell shall not prevail against it."
Amabilis . . . super amorem mulierum (2 Kings 1:26).
"Amiable . . . above the love of women."
Beata, quae credidisti (Lk. 1:45).
"Blessed art thou that hast believed."
Et qui creavit me, requievit in tabernaculo meo (Ecclus. 24:12).
"And He that made me rested in my tabernacle."
Pariet autem Filium, et vocabis nomen ejus Jesum. Ipse enim salvum faciet populum suum (Mt. 1:21).
"And she shall bring forth a Son, and shall call His name Jesus. For He shall

90

	save His people from their sins."
Virgo prudentissima Virgin most prudent	*Eratque mulier illa prudentissima* (1 Kings 25:3). "And she was a prudent . . . woman."
Virgo veneranda Virgin most venerable	*Beatam me dicent omnes generationes* (Lk. 1:48). "All generations shall call me blessed."
Virgo praedicanda Virgin most renowned	*Non recedat laus tua de ore hominum* (Judith 13:25). "Thy praise shall not depart out of the mouth of men."
Virgo potens Virgin most powerful	*In manu tua virtus et potentia* (1 Par. 29:12). "In thy hand is power and might."
Virgo clemens Virgin most merciful	*Clemens ero, in quem mihi placuerit* (Exod. 33:19). "I will be merciful to whom it shall please me."
Virgo fidelis Virgin most faithful	*Esto fidelis usque ad mortem* (Apoc. 2:10). "Be thou faithful unto death."
Speculum justitiae Mirror of justice	*Videmus nunc per speculum* (1 Cor. 13:12). "We see now through a glass."
Sedes sapientiae Seat of wisdom	*Sapientia aedificavit sibi domum, excidit columnas septem* (Prov. 9:1). "Wisdom hath built herself a house, she hath hewn her out seven pillars."
Causa nostrae laetitiae Cause of our joy	*Tristitia (nostra) convertetur in gaudium* (Jn. 16:20). "Our sadness shall be turned into joy."
Vas spirituale Spiritual vessel *Vas honorabile* Vessel of honor	*Vas in honorem* (Rom. 9:21). "A vessel unto honor." *Vas admirabile, opus Excelsi* (Ecclus. 43:2). "An admirable instrument, the work of the Most High."
Vas insigne devotionis Singular vessel of devotion	*Egredietur Vas purissimum* (Prov. 25:4). "There shall come forth a most pure vessel."
Rosa mystica Mystical rose *Turris Davidica* Tower of David	*Coronemus nos rosis* (Wisd. 2:8). "Let us crown ourselves with roses." *Turris fortitudinis a facie inimici* (Ps. 60:4). "A tower of strength against the face of the enemy."
Turris eburnea Tower of ivory	*Fecit etiam Rex Salomon thronum de ebore grandem, et vestivit eum auro fulvo nimis* (3 Kings 10:18).

"King Solomon also made a great throne of ivory, and overlaid it with the finest gold."

Domus aurea
House of gold
Foederis arca
Ark of the covenant

Domus templi ex auro (3 Kings 7:50).
"The house of the temple . . . of gold."
Vir mortis es, sed hodie te non interficiam: quia portasti Arcam Domini (3 Kings 2:26).
"Thou art worthy of death: but I will not at this time put thee to death, because thou didst carry the ark of the Lord."

Janua coeli
Gate of heaven

Attollite portas Principes vestras (Ps. 23:7).
"Lift up your gates, O ye princes."

Stella matutina
Morning star

Stella splendida et matutina (Apoc. 22:16).
"The bright and morning star."

Salus infirmorum
Health of the sick

Virtus exibat . . . et sanabat omnes (Lk. 6:19).
"Virtue went forth . . . and healed all."

Refugium peccatorum
Refuge of sinners

Memor, ero Rahab, et Babylonis scientium me (Ps. 86:4).
"I will be mindful of Rahab, and of Babylon knowing me."

Consolatrix afflictorum
Consoler of the afflicted

Vae, genti insurgenti super genus meum: Dominus enim omnipotens vindicabit in eis (Judith 16:20).
"Woe be to the nation that riseth up against my people: for the Lord almighty will take revenge on them."

Auxilium Christianorum
Help of Christians

Dona mihi . . . populum meum, pro quo obsecro (Esther 7:3).
"Give me . . . my people for which I request."

Regina angelorum
Queen of angels

Dominare nostri tu et Filius tuus (Judges 8:22).
"Rule thou over us, and thy son."

Regina patriarcharum
Queen of patriarchs

Hi patriarchae, et cognationum principes, qui habitaverunt in Jerusalem (1 Par. 8:28).
"These were the chief fathers and heads of their families who dwelt in Jerusalem."

Regina prophetarum
Queen of prophets
Regina Apostolorum
Queen of Apostles

Major est, qui prophetat (1 Cor. 14).
"For greater is he that prophesieth."
Erant perseverantes cum . . . Maria Matre Jesu (Acts 1:14).

92

	"These were persevering with . . . Mary the Mother of Jesus."
Regina martyrum Queen of martyrs	*Et tuam ipsius animam permansibit gladius* (Lk. 2:35). "And thy own soul a sword shall pierce."
Regina confessorum Queen of confessors	*Procidebant . . . ante sedentem in throno . . . et mittebant coronas suas ante thronum* (Apoc. 4:10). "They fell down before Him that sitteth on the throne and . . . cast their crowns before the throne."
Regina Virginum Queen of Virgins	*Virgines enim sunt. Hi sequuntur agnum, quocumque ierit* (Apoc. 14:4). "For they are virgins. These follow the Lamb wheresoever He goeth."
Regina sanctorum omnium Queen of all saints	*Erit mons domus Domini praeparatus in vertice montium* (Mich. 4:1). "The mountain of the house of the Lord shall be prepared in the top of mountains."
Agnus Dei qui tollis peccata mundi Lamb of God, who takest away the sins of the world.	*Et pepercit populo suo* (Joel 2:18). "And (the Lord) . . . hath spared His people."
Agnus Dei qui tollis peccata mundi Lamb of God, who takest away the sins of the world.	*Sic deprecatus exaudietur* (Ecclus. 33:4). "So having prayed, he shall be heard."
Agnus Dei qui tollis peccata mundi Lamb of God, who takest away the sins of the world.	*Deus misereatur nostri et benedicat nobis* (Ps. 66:2). "May God have mercy on us and bless us."

Besides these, the common symbols of the Blessed Virgin are the lily, the rose, and the star. Medieval artists portrayed also the fleece of Gideon (Judges 6:37), but this symbol is always strange to modern eyes. The burning bush from which Jaweh spoke to Moses is also a good symbol of the Blessed Virgin, referring to her perpetual virginity, because as the bush burned and yet was not consumed by the fire, so the Blessed Virgin brought forth a Son without her virginity being in any way impaired. This figure was sometimes found in medieval art. The Blessed Virgin was also represented by

.164.

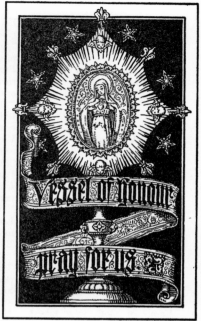

.165.

MA  RIA

.166.

the unicorn, but no example of this is shown here because it is unintelligible to the faithful of our day.

The artist of our day is often called upon for symbols of the Blessed Virgin, and with some ingenuity and liturgical feeling he can produce results which are beautiful both from the decorative standpoint and from the point of theological meaning. The Litany of Loreto alone will supply him with unlimited material.

.166. Under the figure of the orans the Blessed Virgin is represented as praying for the faithful symbolized by the dove resting on the pillar, and for the pagans symbolized by the dove on the broken branch, that they may both reach paradise symbolized by the trees. This figure is taken from a gold glass in the Vatican Museum.

.167. The Blessed Virgin stands with the Christ Child in a vase having four flutings or bays. From the two openings in the vase salvation flows out into the world. The inscription ΜΗΤΗΡ ΘΕΟΥ Η ΠΗΓΗ (*Meter Theou, He Pege*) — "Mother of God, the fountain," indicates that this symbolizes Mary, God's Mother, as the source of salvation. The original of this symbol is found on a cut stone now in the Museo Vettori, Rome.

95

.167.

.168.

.172.

.173.

.174.

.169.

.177.

.170.

.168.–.172. Monograms of the name *Maria* (Mary) in various arrangements. In .168., .170., and .171. the full name is contained. .171., coming from the eighteenth century, is especially ingenious. The monogram is formed by olive branches, symbol of peace. The olives clinging to the branches remind us of the fact that in ancient times their oil was used for healing wounds, and that Jesus, Fruit of the womb of the Virgin Mary, healed the wounds of the world made by sin.

.173. The root of Jesse (Isa. 11:1).
.174. The cedar on the hill.
.175. The enclosed garden (Cant. 4:12).
.176. The sealed fountain (Cant. 4:12).
.177. The sealed book (Isa. 29:11).

96

.171.

.175.

.176.

.178.–.181. Various conceptions of the sacred heart of Mary.

.182.–.183. The lily, symbol of Mary's purity, as represented during medieval times. This form is also called the *fleur de lis.*

.184. The mirror of purity.

.185. The lily among thorns.

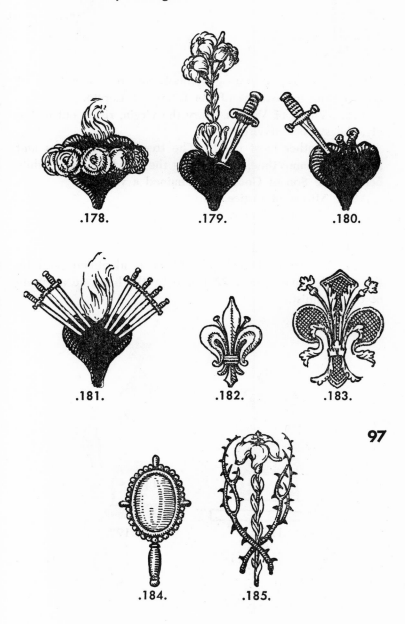

.178.   .179.   .180.

.181.   .182.   .183.

.184.   .185.

97

.188.

.189.

.190.

.186.

These and the following symbols are representations of some of the invocations of the Litany of Loreto.

.186. Virgin of Virgins. Mary the virgin, rising out of the lily, the symbol of virginity.

.187. Mother most chaste. The tree bears blossoms and fruit at the same time, symbolizing the fact that Mary, while bearing the Son of God, still remained a virgin.

.188. Mirror of justice.

.189. Vessel of honor.

.190. Spiritual vessel.

.191. Seat of wisdom.

.192. Tower of David. The tower is identified both by the star of David (see **.127.**), and by the harp, an attribute of the Psalmist.

98

.187.

.191.

.192.

.197.

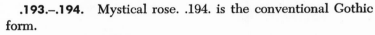

.198.

.193.

.194.

.193.–.194. Mystical rose. .194. is the conventional Gothic form.

.195. Tower of ivory.

.196. House of gold.

.197. Ark of the covenant.

.198. Gate of heaven. Note the IHC, the symbol of Christ, union with whom is the reward of the faithful in heaven.

.199. Help of Christians.

.200. Morning star.

.201. Queen of virgins.

99

.195.

.199.

.200.

.201.

.196.

.202.

.203.

.204.

.202. Mother of our Creator.
.203. Virgin of virgins.
.204. Help of Christians.
.205. Tower of David.
.206. Morning star.

100

.205.

.206.

.207.

11. THE ECCLESIASTICAL YEAR

SYMBOLS of the seasons of the ecclesiastical year are useful
for the ornamentation of small articles, such as greeting cards,
calendars, and the like, and even in large-scale decorations.
The best possibility for symbolization arises from a consideration of the seasons in connection with the life of the Savior.
Christmas represents His coming upon earth; Easter, His

101

glorious resurrection from the dead; Pentecost, the coming of the Holy Spirit to confirm and strengthen the leaders whom He had chosen for His Church on earth.

For Christmas the figures of the Christ Child, the crib, the star of the Magi, or the IHS serve very well as symbols. These are probably the most commonly seen and the most understandable although there are others equally appropriate and meaningful such as the mystical rose (see .194.) and the blossoming rod. There is one very early Christmas sym-

.208.

bol, found in the cemetery of St. Sebastian in Rome, an adaptation of which is shown on page 101. This picture comes from sometime in the fourth century and is probably the oldest symbolic conception, or picture, of the nativity of our Savior. The picture shows a kind of table or bench on which lies a child wrapped in swaddling clothes. Beside the Infant

102

stand an ox and an ass, their heads close to His as though breathing upon Him. Above the Child is the bust picture of a young man, with a nimbus, a typical fourth-century representation of our Savior. This serves to identify the symbolic picture below.

The ox and ass have their own significance, and tradition is fairly constant in affirming their presence in the stable at the birth of Christ. According to the story they warmed the Infant Savior with their breath, and as though to bear this out all early pictures show them with heads close to the Child's. Symbolic meaning is given to them, the ox representing the Jews who were under the yoke of the Old Law, and the ass the pagans. St. Augustine, however, considers the ox the symbol of the shepherds and the ass the symbol of the Magi. An apocryphal gospel of the first century after Christ also mentions these animals.

For Easter, besides the representation of the Lamb carrying the banner of the resurrection (the white pennant with red cross, affixed to a cruciform staff), every symbol of the Savior is appropriate which represents Him as Victor over death.

Pentecost is beautifully symbolized by the dove of the Holy Spirit with the seven flames or seven lamps, representing His seven gifts.

12. THE FOUR LAST THINGS

THE artist will sometimes be called upon for symbols of the four last things. It will be quite necessary for him, if he is to present these subjects properly, to grasp the true Christian philosophy of death and suffering. The usual symbols of death, the skull and crossbones and the hourglass with the sand run out, both represent death as the end of life — as a mere negative thing, and as something ugly and terrifying. Christian philosophy, on the other hand, looks upon death as the beginning of life, as the liberation of the soul from the earthly prison of the body. It is aptly symbolized by the representation of the bird escaping from the cage into the brightness of the skies, an idea drawn from the Psalms (67:19).

Pictures of birds and cages are found in the catacombs, and while experts consider them as referring to Christ in the womb of His Blessed Mother, a view that is strengthened by the addition, in one case at least, of the words of Isaias (7:14), some of them may refer also to the soul held within the prison of the body. The same idea is embodied in the picture of the butterfly escaping from the cocoon. This idea is most beautiful and lends itself well to decorative purposes, but it lacks the backing of any long tradition.

The judgment which the soul of man must undergo at death is a balancing of the soul in the scales of eternity. There seems to be no tradition for the representation of the scales in this connection, but the idea comes from pre-Christian times. One of the few symbolic pictures of the last

104

judgment is that by Memling, in the Church of the Blessed Virgin, in Danzig. The idea of it is drawn from the Apocalypse: God is shown seated on His throne; from one side of His mouth proceeds a sword and from the other a lily. Below is the Archangel Michael weighing souls on a scale. This is very significant, but it is a picture rather than a symbol, and hence of slight value for ordinary use.

Heaven was beautifully symbolized in the early ages of our era, especially on the early tombstones. The crown, the palms, the dove holding in its beak the crown of laurel, all of these represent heaven, the reward of the faithful.

The subject of hell is a disagreeable one for which there are few fitting symbols. The gates of hell might be shown in the form of the gaping jaws of a lion, an idea found in the offertory of the Mass for the dead, *Libera eos de ore leonis*, "Deliver them from the jaws of the lion." Another symbol may be found in the four rivers of Hades of pagan mythology. The rivers are Acheron, Styx, Kokytos, and Phlegeton. They might be used in a symbolic design in contrast to the rivers symbolizing the four Gospels.

The symbols shown on the following pages will help the artist in devising suitable designs.

.209. This rather curious symbol of death was found on an old tombstone. The wagon of life stands motionless. The tongue of the wagon forms a cross and lays back as though protecting and bringing peace to the soul, represented by the object covered with the cloth.

.210. Another symbol of death, the bird escaping from the cage.

.211. The scales balanced on the sword of justice.

105

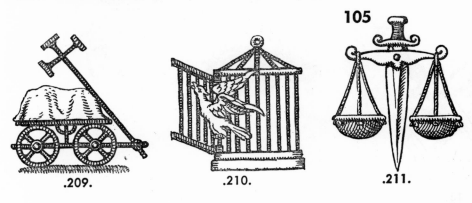

.209.   .210.   .211.

.212. The scales balanced on the cross. The jewels, representing the things of earth, are outweighed by the cross, the anchor, and the crown of thorns, representing the virtues and sufferings of the faithful soul.

.213. A symbol of the punishments of hell.

.214. The butterfly emerging from its cocoon represents death, the passing from a circumscribed life to the more complete and beautiful life of heaven.

.215. Death in Christ, represented by the cross, brings the crown and palms of eternal life. The cross in this symbol is evidence that the device is of late origin.

.216. The soul of the faithful, the dove, receives its reward, the laurel crown, and everlasting peace, the olive branch.

.217. The hand of God confers the crown and palm of eternal life in the name of Christ (the cross).

.218. The rewards of the faithful in heaven above the stars are the crown and palms of victory.

106

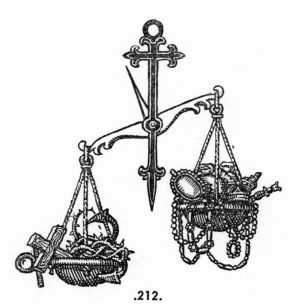

.212.

.213.

.214.

.215.

.216.

.217.

.218.

107

INDEX

Abstract ideas, 17
Adonai, 27
Alpha-omega, 23, 32, 33, 43
Anchor, 31, 42
Anchor cross, 38
Andrew, St., 58
Antependium, decoration of, 73
Apostles, 56 ff
Ark and rainbow, symbol of
  Church, 63, 68
Art, supernatural in, 15
Attribute, meaning of, 16

Baptism, symbols of, 74 ff
Bartholomew, St., 59
Beehive, symbol of Church, 63, 67
Bird, symbol, 105
Books, four, as symbol of Church,
  61
Bush, burning, symbol of B.V.M.,
  93
Butterfly, 107

Candle, symbol of Trinity, 24
Candles, three, 24
Chalice, and book, symbol, 86;
  symbol, 85
Christ, two natures in, symbols, 45
Christmas, symbols of, 102
Christogram, 23, 31, 32, 39, 44,
  46; enthroned, 43
Church, the, 60 ff; personification
  of, 63
Circles, interlaced, 23; symbol of
  infinity, 22
Confirmation, symbols of, 76
Constantine, emperor, 33
Creed, articles of, and Apostles, 58
Cross, before fifth century, 30;
  Celtic, 31, 39; disguised, 30;
  papal, 38; patriarchal, 38

Crown, 107
Crucifix, 16
Crux ansata, 38
Crux dissimulata, 30
Crux gemmata, 31, 38

Death, symbols of, 104 f
Dextera Domini, 27; symbol of
  Father, 25
Dove, 107; symbol of baptism, 81;
  symbol of Holy Spirit, 48
Doves, 43

Eagle, symbol, 51; symbol of bap-
  tism, 82; symbol of Holy Spirit,
  48
Easter, symbol of, 103
Easter banner, 37, 46
Ecclesiastical year, 101 ff
El Shaddai, 27
Eucharist, *see* Holy Eucharist
Euphrates, river, 51
Evangelists, 50 ff; symbols, 52, 53,
  54, 55; *see also* Matthew; Mark;
  Luke; John; Gospels
Extreme Unction, symbol, 86
Eye, all-seeing, 22, 26, 27

Father, God the, earliest symbols
  of, 25; symbol from Old Testa-
  ment, 25
Fish, 40, 42; as symbol, 35; sym-
  bol of baptism, 81; symbol of
  Holy Eucharist, 82, 83; symbol-
  ism of, 72
Fishes, three, 24
Fleece of Gideon, symbol of
  B.V.M., 93
Fountain, symbol, 95
Four last things, 104 ff

Gishon (Gehon, Gihon), river, 51
Glory, *see* Mandorla
God, names of, in Old Testament, 26
Gospels, 50 ff; symbol, 52
Grapes, symbol, 85
Greek, use of, in early symbols, 32
Griffin, 45

Hands, clasped, symbol, 86
Heaven, symbols of, 107
Hell, symbol, 106
Holy Eucharist, symbols of, 77 f, 82 ff
Holy Orders, symbol, 86; symbols of, 80
Holy Spirit, 48 ff; gifts of, 49; human representation of, 48
Holy Trinity, *see* Trinity, Holy
Hourglass, symbol, 86

IHC, 34, 40, 41
IHS, *see* IHC
Israel, tribes of, 68, 69, 70

James the Greater, St., 58
James the Less, St., 58
John, St., 58; symbol of, 51
John Chrysostom, 31
Jude, St., 59
Judgment, symbols of, 104 f

Keys, symbol, 85

Labarum, 33, 43
Lamb, 44, 46; as symbol, 37
Lamb and book, 46
Lambs, as symbols of Apostles, 57
Lily, symbol of B.V.M., 93
Lion, symbol, 51
Litany of Loreto, 88 ff; symbols of, 96 ff
Luke, St., symbol of, 51

Man, winged, 51
Mandorla, 20
Mark, St., symbol of, 51
Mary, Blessed Virgin, 87 ff; monograms of, 96
Matrimony, symbols of, 80

Matthew, St., 59; symbol of, 51
Matthias, St., 59
Monogram of Jesus, 40
Moses, in symbol of Church, 61

Nimbus, color of, 19; of divine Persons, 19; meaning of, 18; in middle ages, 20

Old Testament, names of God in, 22
Orans, 88, 95
Orpheus, as symbol, 38
Ox (bull), symbol, 51

Palms, 107
Palm tree, 45
Paradise, rivers of, 50
Passion, instruments of, 38, 47
Paul, St., symbol of, 59
Peacock, 47; as symbol, 34
Pelican, symbol, 85
Penance, symbols of, 79
Pentecost, symbols of, 103
Peter, St., 58; in symbol of Church, 65
Philip, St., 58
Phison (Pishon, Pison), river, 51
Phoenix, 45, 47
Pillar, symbol of Church, 62, 65, 66
Prototype, 16

Rainbow, *see* Ark
Resurrection banner, *see* Easter banner
Rings, symbol, 86
Rivers, four, of Paradise, 50
Rock, symbol of Church, 60
Rose, symbol of B.V.M., 93

Sacraments, 71 ff
Sacred Heart, 46, 47; symbol, 38; symbol, restrictions in use of, 38
St. Peter's, symbol of Church, 68
Scales, symbol, 105, 106
Scourge, symbol, 85
Scripture, use of, in symbols, 73
Serpent, 43: brazen, 45
Shamrock, 22, 24